MW01285001

Analytical Grammar

Level 5
Punctuation and Usage
Instructor Handbook

Created by R. Robin Finley

**ANALYTICAL
GRAMMAR.**

888-854-6284
analyticalgrammar.com
customerservice@demmelearning.com

Analytical Grammar: Level 5, Punctuation and Usage Instructor Handbook
© 1996 R. Robin Finley
© 2022 Demme Learning, Inc.
Published and distributed by Demme Learning

All rights reserved. No part of this book may be reproduced, stored in a retrieval system, or transmitted in any form by any means—electronic, mechanical, photocopying, recording, or otherwise—without prior written permission from Demme Learning.

analyticalgrammar.com

1-888-854-6284 or 1-717-283-1448 | demmelearning.com
Lancaster, Pennsylvania USA

ISBN 978-1-60826-599-2
Revision Code 1122

Printed in the United States of America by CJK Group
 2 3 4 5 6 7 8 9 10

For information regarding CPSIA on this printed material call: 1-888-854-6284
and provide reference # 1122-11012022

Table of Contents

Level 5 | Punctuation and Usage

Why We Learn Grammar

Children begin learning the grammar of their native language long before they can speak it fluently. Even a toddler knows that "Dad ate pizza" makes sense, while "Pizza ate dad" is silly! Unlike other subjects, we already know the grammar of our daily language—even if we don't know that we know it. The key, therefore, is two-fold:

- Apply labels to the different parts of speech and grammar. We know grammar; we just may not know the names of things or why they are organized in certain ways.

- Understand how to use different language and grammar in different situations. While formal situations call for more formal language, the grammar of our everyday, informal language is not incorrect. Correct grammar changes depending on the situation. Just as a person using informal slang might be judged in a formal business setting, the opposite is true: using formal language in an environment where casual language is the norm would seem strange.

These two components combine to make us better writers and, therefore, better communicators. Consistent use of grammar and proper use of punctuation helps keep written information flowing easily to the reader. With a mature understanding of grammar, students are better able to share their increasingly complex thoughts and ideas in a clear, understandable way.

Getting Started

Some grammar "rules" are unbreakable. A sentence must always have a subject and a verb, for example. However, in many cases, rather than "rules," they should be looked at as "guidelines." Even professional grammarians (We do exist!) disagree on things like what a prepositional phrase is modifying in a sentence. Sometimes we even disagree with ourselves from day to day! This is okay. A sentence can be grammatically correct even if there is disagreement about how it is parsed or diagrammed. If your student has enough grammar knowledge to make an informed argument as to why they believe a certain answer is correct, it's a win—give them credit and move on.

The goal of each lesson is that students acquire enough familiarity with the topic that they can achieve 80% on the assessment. *Analytical Grammar* is intended to be an open-book curriculum, meaning that students are encouraged to use the lesson notes to complete all exercises and assessments, so this should not be a difficult goal if students are completing the exercises. Once a level is completed, the lesson notes and Application & Enrichment pages are designed to be removed from the book to create a grammar handbook that the student can use for life.

Grammar is a cumulative process. While new parts of speech will be addressed in subsequent lessons, students will continue to practice what they have already learned, and new skills will build upon that knowledge.

Analytical Grammar is just one component of a complete language arts program, which should include literature, writing, and vocabulary or spelling. By dividing the program into five levels, students are able to spend a short time focusing on grammar, then concentrate more fully on another component armed with the skills to improve their communication. Completing a reinforcement activity every couple of weeks and using the review lesson, when available, prior to starting the next level ensures that students' skills stay sharp.

Components

Analytical Grammar is separated into five levels

Level 1: Grammar Basics: elementary introduction to the nine parts of speech.

Level 2: Mechanics: elementary guidelines for punctuation and word usage.

Level 3: Parts of Speech: complex information about parts of speech and their interactions

Level 4: Phrases and Clauses: advanced work with more complex components

Level 5: Punctuation and Usage: in-depth information about punctuation and word usage

For each level, you will need these components:

Student Worktext

- *Student Notes* provide instruction and examples for each topic
- *Exercises A, B, and C* give students plenty of practice in applying their new knowledge
- *Application & Enrichment* activities provide weekly instruction and practice with functional writing skills
- *Assessments* are always open book and provide an accurate measure of proficiency
- *Reinforcement* worksheets are provided to keep skills sharp between levels

Instructor's Handbook

- Page-by-page Student Worktext copy with solutions for all student work
- Instructor tips with additional explanation on possible points of confusion
- Item-by-item scoring guide for all assessments

29-Week Schedule

The study of grammar is just one part of a complete language arts program. Your student is expected to progress through the Analytical Grammar lessons at their own pace, then continue to practice grammar skills while studying another area of Language Arts.

Review

Week 1	Review

Lessons

Week 2	Lesson 1
Week 3	Lesson 2
Week 4	Lesson 3
Week 5	Lesson 4
Week 6	Lesson 5
Week 7	Lesson 6
Week 8	Lesson 7
Week 9	Lesson 8
Week 10	Lesson 9
Week 11	Lesson 10
Week 12	Lesson 11
Week 13	Lesson 12
Week 14	Lesson 13
Week 15	Lesson 14
Week 16	Lesson 15
Week 17	Lesson 16
Week 18	Lesson 17
Week 19	Lesson 18
Week 20	Lesson 19

High School Grammar Reinforcement

Week 21	Reinforcement
Week 22	Break
Week 23	Reinforcement
Week 24	Break
Week 25	Reinforcement
Week 26	Break
Week 27	Reinforcement
Week 28	Break
Week 29	Reinforcement

Reinforcing Skills

Once Level 5 is completed, your student will have learned everything they need to know about grammar! Well, maybe not quite—there are always quirky rules or situations that will come up. But they will be armed with the knowledge they need to communicate their ideas clearly and effectively in any situation.

To keep their skills sharp, consider our *High School Grammar Reinforcements*. These self-corrected workbooks provide practice activities based on common high school literature themes. *World Authors*, *American Authors*, *British Authors*, and *Shakespeare's Plays* do not have to be used with literature, but they provide interesting background information on important authors and literary works. Complete one activity every two weeks during the school year to keep students at the top of their grammar game.

An *Analytical Grammar* Week

Most *Analytical Grammar* lessons are set up in the same manner: a page of notes, three exercises, an Application and Enrichment activity, and an assessment. The following is a suggested schedule for completing one lesson a week.

Monday

Read over the lesson notes with your student.

Have your student **complete Exercise A**.

- Work the first one or two sentences together, then have your student complete the rest. Remind them that they can use the lesson notes as needed throughout the week. Encourage them to ask for as much help as they need.

Tuesday

Review Exercise A.

This should take no more than 20 minutes.

Discuss only those mistakes that relate to the lesson you are working on.

Have your student **complete Exercise B**.

Wednesday

Review Exercise B.

Have your student **complete Exercise C**.

Thursday

Review Exercise C.

Read over and discuss the Application & Enrichment activity.

Have your student **complete the Application & Enrichment activity**.

- Note that Application & Enrichment activities include important concepts for grammar proficiency, so don't skip them.

Friday

Review the Application & Enrichment activity.

Have your student **complete the assessment**.*

- Remind them that it is open book and they should use the lesson notes as much as necessary.

Some lessons in Level 5 do not have an individual assessment; rather, there is a cumulative assessment every three or four lessons.

The following Monday

Correct the assessment together.

- You read out the answers as your student crosses out any incorrect answers.

- Then, using the scoring guide found in the Instructor's Handbook on the assessment key, total up the correct answers and record the score on the test.

Now, **introduce the next lesson** and start the process all over again!

Potential Activities

Parsing

There are only nine parts of speech. Some parts will always have the same job in a sentence. Others can fill a variety of roles depending on how they are used. Identifying the parts of speech helps to narrow down the roles they may play. You will never find an adjective acting as an object, for example. Adjectives are always modifiers. On the other hand, nouns can do many different jobs in a sentence. Identifying parts of speech is called parsing. This is the first step to identifying the job that a word is doing in a sentence, since it helps students narrow down the possibilities.

art   adj   adj   n   av   pp   art   n   pp   art   n

Example: The quick brown fox jumped (over the dog) (in the road).

Short Answers and Fill-in-the-Blanks

Some exercises include short answer and fill-in-the-blank questions. These include activities like providing definitions, identifying a word's job in a sentence, and revising sentences to have proper punctuation.

Diagramming and "The Process"

Diagramming a sentence can strike fear into even the most experienced grammar student. That's why we break it down into an easy-to-follow series of questions that we call "The Process." In small increments, by answering yes/no questions about the sentence, students learn to diagram increasingly complex sentences until they are confidently creating elaborate diagrams. Your student will be well prepared for the challenge. Some students enjoy the satisfaction of putting all of the parts of a sentence into their proper places.

We don't, however, diagram just for the sake of it. Diagramming visually demonstrates the structure of a sentence. It can clarify a relationship between two parts of speech like no amount of words can. While it is important to practice each new skill learned, once a student can demonstrate confidence with the part of speech, diagramming can be reduced, and you may find that your student doesn't need to complete every sentence in every exercise. It is simply a tool to support understanding of the parts that make up a sentence's structure. By Level 5, when grammar concepts are secondary to punctuation rules and guidelines, diagramming is put aside, but the knowledge acquired remains.

Application & Enrichment

On the fourth day of each lesson, students will complete an Application & Enrichment activity. These activities are based on grammar, punctuation, and writing skills. They aren't usually directly related to the topic of the lesson, but they cover important concepts that will benefit students as they develop their writing skills. These activities provide a break from the lesson content, allowing students' brains an opportunity to store the grammar information they are learning in long-term memory. While these activities are intended to be fun and informative, they introduce and practice important skills and should not be skipped.

Assessment

On the fifth day of a lesson, students have an opportunity to show you and themselves what they have learned. They will be asked to complete exercises that are similar to the daily exercises. Points are assigned to each section; they are found in the Instructor's Handbook with the solutions. The points are intended to be a measuring stick for how confident the student feels about the material. Remember, your student can use their lesson notes to complete the assessment. They should not try to complete it from memory, without support. Before moving to the next lesson, the goal is for your student to receive at least 80% on the assessment. If your student scores less than 80%, we recommend you review that lesson's notes with them before introducing the next topic and provide heavier support as they begin the new lesson's exercises.

Notes on correcting assessments

When tallying assessment points, be sure to count the number correct. Don't count the number of errors and subtract that from the given number of total points. As your student acquires their grammar knowledge, they may mark a part of speech that shouldn't be marked in a particular lesson. Do not count these misplaced marks as incorrect. This problem will resolve itself in time as they progress through the program.

For assessments with diagrams, you will notice that the diagrams in the solutions have check marks indicating what should be counted as a "point." Go through your student's diagram item by item and compare the checked items. If an item is in the correct place, make a checkmark. If it's in the wrong place, circle it so that your student can see where they made a mistake.

For modifiers, if they are attached to the correct word and diagrammed correctly, count them as correct even if the word they are modifying is in the wrong place.

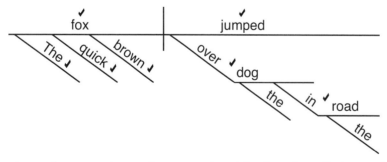

Example: The quick brown fox jumped (over the dog) (in the road).

This diagram is worth seven points. Points are assigned for the subject (fox), verb (jumped), fox's modifiers (The, quick, and brown), the prepositional phrase attached to "jumped" (over the dog), and the prepositional phrase attached to "dog" (in the road). Notice that although the prepositional phrases have three words, they each only have one check mark and therefore are worth one point as a unit.

Now imagine your student diagrammed the sentence like this:

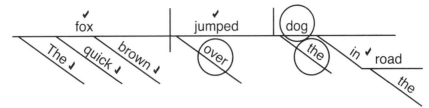

This diagram only loses one point. The prepositional phrase over the dog was only worth one point, so therefore it can only lose one point if it's incorrectly diagrammed. The prepositional phrase in the road is still correct and earns one point because it is correctly attached to *dog*.

Tips for Success

This course can be adapted to meet your student's needs.

- If your student is confident, consider allowing them to "test out" of a lesson. Have them look over the lesson notes and, if they feel ready, take the lesson assessment. If the student scores at least 80% correct on the assessment, skip to the next lesson. They will still get plenty of practice with the skipped concept.

- If a lesson feels overwhelming and your student needs to slow down a little, have them do the odd sentences in an exercise one day and the evens the next.

- Consider only asking your student to diagram half of the sentences in an exercise. If they understand the concept and can identify the word, phrase, or clause that is the focus of the lesson, they do not necessarily need to diagram every sentence.

- On the other hand, encourage students to diagram at least one or two sentences from each lesson. Diagramming creates a visual image of how parts of speech interact. Allow them to choose which sentences they would like to diagram.

- Remind your student that they should look at the lesson notes for help as they are completing the exercises and even the assessment.

Lesson 1
Comma Errors

About *Punctuation and Usage*

After studying grammar guidelines in detail in Levels 3 and 4, it's time to change the focus to punctuation and usage. Understanding specific grammar constructions will help students to understand when and how to use punctuation properly. Writing is how we communicate in many situations, and communication is more than just sending a message. The message also needs to be received and understood, and proper punctuation helps to guide the receiver by removing obstacles to understanding.

Analytical Grammar Level 5: Punctuation and Usage does not include Instructor Notes. Your student's familiarity with grammar means that they are not necessary beyond this point. Continue to review the Student Notes with your student and be available to work through any questions with them.

A Tip for Instructors

If your student confidently completes Exercise A independently and without error, you may skip Exercises B and C and give them the option of taking the assessment early. If they score at least an 80% on the assessment, they are ready to move on. Decide with your student whether to jump into the next lesson immediately, or take a short break and wait for the following Monday. Either way, your student should still complete that lesson's Application & Enrichment activity before moving on.

Lesson 1: Comma Errors

In Level 3, you were introduced to these common comma mistakes that can detract from your ideas. Let's review the places you **don't** need commas before we learn the rules about where you **do** need them.

Commas are a common source of error in punctuation, but they don't need to be if we pay attention to sentence structure as we write. There are rules for where a comma should be used, and there are rules for where a comma should never be used!

Every time you place a comma, make sure you know **why** you are putting it there!

There are two main kinds of comma errors: **comma splices** and **comma splits.**

Comma splice

To splice is to join two things together so that they become one thing. For example, two ropes can be spliced together by weaving the strands of one rope with strands from the other so that the two parts become one rope.

A **comma splice** is when you use a comma to join two sentences. Comma splices are sometimes called **run-on sentences,** and it's easy to see why. Look at this example:

> **Example:** We spent the whole day at the beach, we had the sunburn to prove it!

We spent the whole day at the beach and *we had the sunburn to prove it* are both independent clauses. They are complete sentences on their own, so we have two sentences that run together with no clear starting or stopping point. There are several ways we could fix this problem.

1) Just write two separate sentences:
We spent the whole day at the beach. We had the sunburn to prove it!

2) Join the sentences with a comma and a conjunction, such as *and*:
We spent the whole day at the beach, and we had the sunburn to prove it!

3) Join the sentences with a subordinating conjunction, such as *since* (*Phrases and Clauses*, Lesson 6):
Since we spent the whole day at the beach, we had the sunburn to prove it!

4) Join the two sentences with a semicolon (*Punctuation and Usage*, Lesson 10):
We spent the whole day at the beach; we had the sunburn to prove it!

Comma split

This is the opposite of a comma splice. Rather than incorrectly joining two sentences, a **comma split** incorrectly divides a sentence. It is a single comma that comes between two words, phrases, or clauses that shouldn't be separated. Here is a list of places where a comma should never be:

1) There should never be only one comma between the **subject** and **verb.**

> **Example:** Incorrect: The butler carrying a tray, walked into the room.
> Correct: The butler, carrying a tray, walked into the room.
> Also correct: Carrying a tray, the butler walked into the room.

2) There should never be only one comma separating a **verb** and its **direct object.**

> **Example:** Incorrect: We discovered after searching carefully, many things.
> Correct: We discovered, after searching carefully, many things.

3) There should never be only one comma separating a **linking verb** and its **complement** (its predicate adjective or predicate nominative).

> **Example:** Incorrect: James felt, absolutely wonderful.
> Correct: James felt absolutely wonderful.

4) There should never be only one comma separating a **modifier** and its **noun.** If there is more than one adjective, there should be no comma between the final one that is closest to the noun.

> **Example:** Incorrect: The soft, cuddly, sweater was gorgeous.
> Correct: The soft, cuddly sweater was gorgeous.

5) There should never be only one comma separating a **verb** and its **indirect object.**

> **Example:** Incorrect: I wrote, my aunt in Florida a letter.
> Correct: I wrote my aunt in Florida a letter.

6) There should never be only one comma separating an **indirect object** and its **direct object.**

> **Example:** Incorrect: I wrote my aunt in Florida, a letter.
> Correct: I wrote my aunt in Florida a letter.

Why do we emphasize that there shouldn't be only one comma? Because, if there is a clause or phrase in the middle of the sentence that should be set apart, it will have two commas—just like this sentence does! You will learn the rules about how and when to place commas around non-essential modifiers and other "interrupters" in the next lessons.

Always know **why** you are placing a comma in a sentence. Remember that nonessential information in the middle of a sentence needs to have commas on both ends. And remember the no-no splits!

1) subject and verb

2) verb and direct object

3) linking verb and complement

4) modifier and its noun

5) verb and indirect object

6) indirect object and direct object

Comma Errors: Exercise A

Directions

Rewrite the following sentences to remove the comma splice.

Answers will vary.

1) The birds love to gather at the bird feeder, they chatter all day to one another.

The birds love to gather at the bird feeder, and they chatter all day to one another.

2) The garden needs to be weeded, it's hard to see the flowers!

The garden needs to be weeded. It's hard to see the flowers!

3) Juan has been working out a lot, is he turning into a gym rat?

Juan has been working out a lot. Is he turning into a gym rat?

Directions

Each of the following sentences includes a comma split. Circle the incorrect comma. Write what the comma is splitting below the sentence.

Example: The big, white, woolly, dog looks like a polar bear!

splits modifier (woolly) and its noun (dog)

4) Violet is the softest, sweetest, black, cat.

splits modifier (black) and its noun (cat)

5) The new quarterback, gives the team a great chance to win this season.

splits subject (quarterback) and verb (gives)

6) This marching band is, very talented!
splits linking verb (is) and predicate adjective (talented)
Note: splits linking verb and complement *is also correct*

7) The poems of Shel Silverstein give everyone, a great deal of joy.

splits indirect object (everyone) and direct object (joy)

8) Why did I wait until the hottest day to mow, the yard?

splits verb (to mow) and direct object (yard)

9) We should buy, Mom a shiny, new, blue car.

splits verb (buy) and indirect object (Mom)

10) Maria's, dress is perfect for this special, exciting occasion!

splits modifier (Maria's) and its noun (dress)

Comma Errors: Exercise B

Directions

Each of the following sentences includes a comma split. Circle the incorrect comma. Write what the comma is splitting below the sentence.

1) Knitting is, an ancient way of making cloth that is still practiced around the world.
   splits linking verb (is) *and complement/predicate nominative* (way)

2) Knitters only need, two or more needles and yarn to get started.
   splits verb (need) *and direct object* (needles and yarn)

3) The way that the yarn is pulled through loops on the needles, creates stitches.
   splits subject (way) *and verb* (creates)

4) These interlocked, stitches are connected into rows.
   splits modifier (interlocked) *and its noun* (stitches)

5) The kind of fabric made by knitting, depends on the yarn and the needles.
   splits subject (kind) *and verb* (depends)

6) To make warm, strong, socks, finely spun wool on small needles is best.
   splits modifier (strong) *and its noun* (socks)

7) Cotton can make you, cool, comfortable summer clothes.
   splits indirect object (you) *and direct object* (clothes)

8) Thick alpaca wool on large needles makes, a soft, warm blanket.
   splits verb (makes) *and direct object* (blanket)

9) Knitting is, a skill shared by many kinds of people and cultures around the world.
   splits linking verb (is) *and complement/predicate nominative* (skill)

10) Knitters show, others their love when they share their knitted creations.
    splits verb (show) *and indirect object* (others)

Comma Errors: Exercise C

Directions

Each of the following sentences includes a comma split. Circle the incorrect comma. Write what the comma is splitting below the sentence.

1) Maria threw John, the football, and he dove to catch it.

    splits indirect object (John) *and direct object* (football)

2) The old, beat-up, rusty, car rattled its way down the street.

    splits modifier (rusty) *and its noun* (car)

3) Mom was, appreciative of her thoughtful Mother's Day gift.

    splits linking verb (was) *and complement/predicate adjective* (appreciative)

4) The holiday decorations, sparkled invitingly above the crackling fire.

    splits subject (decorations) *and verb* (sparkled)

5) Anya gave me her email address so I could send, her my notes.

    splits verb (send) *and indirect object* (her)

6) All the neighbors got together to throw, a big neighborhood party.

    splits verb (to throw) *and direct object* (party)

7) Cool days, warm sweaters, and colorful leaves are, the best parts of fall.

    splits linking verb (are) *and complement/predicate nominative* (parts)

8) Throw the horse, some hay.

    splits indirect object (horse) *and direct object* (hay)

9) After the concert was finished, the band, came back to play one more song

    splits subject (band) *and verb* (came)

10) Many of the chemistry students memorized, the elements for extra credit.

    splits verb (memorized) *and direct object* (elements)

Application & Enrichment

The Point of Punctuation

We might think that punctuation and writing go hand in hand, but that hasn't always been the case. Until the invention of the printing press, many cultures shared two common traits: very few people could read, and writing materials were expensive and rare. Writing existed for thousands of years in many cultures without any punctuation at all. Words and sentences ran together with no spaces, no capital letters to show their beginnings, and no periods to mark their endings. Over the centuries, the few people who could read had a difficult time making sense of it!

In Ancient Greece, writing was mainly for actors, singers, and orators who performed the written material for illiterate citizens to hear. These performers spent a lot of time struggling through the text, which not only lacked punctuation but also had no spaces between words. They would mark the text with their own symbols so they knew when to pause (and for how long) and what to emphasize. There was no uniformity because these breaks were up to each performer's artistic interpretation.

Later, in Medieval Europe, many monks found Latin challenging to read and began inserting spaces between the words. Scribes also began putting their own marks in the text as they copied; they wanted to preserve what was written and prevent others from applying different interpretations. As standards for writing music developed, composers included symbols showing pauses and emphasis for the music and occasionally applied the same marks to the written verses. But still, without any widespread standards, punctuation remained little more than an individual writer's notes.

When the printing press was invented in the 1430s, writing changed. With the production of larger quantities of books, the punctuation repeatedly chosen by printers became the standard over just a few decades. Punctuation marks have changed very little in the centuries since.

Today, we use punctuation similarly to how those ancient Greeks, Medieval monks, and early musicians did: to guide readers with pauses and stops. Even now, some punctuation rules, like some grammar rules, are more like guidelines, and it is left up to the writer to decide how they will guide their readers. Punctuation has a lot of power; it is used to give meaning to groups of words. The following activity will show you the power of punctuation in creating meaning.

Directions

Word-for-word, the two letters below are precisely the same. Their only differences are in punctuation and capitalization. Read each letter while paying particular attention to where the letter writer is asking the reader to pause and stop. Next, circle the punctuation and capitalization differences you find while comparing the two letters. Think about how these differences lead to two very different stories being told. Finally, draw a picture or write 2–3 sentences to tell where the tiger is in each of the letters.

Lead a conversation about the ways that punctuation has changed the meaning between these two letters.

1) Dear Rosie,

Today we learned about wild animals while sitting and watching a movie. In the woods, during an exciting scene, a large angry tiger crossed the screen. Right in front of us was this terrifying creature ready to charge! We then watched it swiftly chase a bear away!

Your friend,

Erin

2) Dear Rosie,

Today we learned about wild animals. While sitting and watching a movie in the woods, during an exciting scene, a large angry tiger crossed the screen right in front of us. Was this terrifying creature ready to charge? We then watched it chase a bear away!

Your friend,

Erin

Letter 1	Letter 2

_____

_____

_____

_____

Comma Rules 1, 2, and 3

A Tip for Instructors

If a lesson seems overwhelming, slow the pace a bit and have your student split up each exercise by doing the odd-numbered sentences one day and even-numbered the next. This will give your student two weeks to complete the lesson instead of one.

Lesson 2: Comma Rules 1, 2, and 3

If punctuation marks are like traffic signs for writing, then it's important to have these signs in the right place. After all, if you decided to put a stop sign in the middle of an interstate highway, you could cause an accident! A lack of speed limit signs could be exciting, but not necessarily in a good way. Just like traffic signs, there are rules about when you need punctuation. Most of us understand when to use a period, question mark, or exclamation mark. Commas, however, can be confusing to even experienced writers. Since we are familiar with grammar guidelines, it is much easier to identify when and where we need commas when we are writing. There are eleven rules for when to use commas. To help us remember them all, each rule has its own "buzzword," or hint. Let's get started!

Comma Rule 1: Items in a Series

Use commas to separate items in a series, or list, that are grammatical equals.

Examples: John, Uncle Hank, Aunt Jean, Sofia, and the dog went swimming. (nouns)

The happy, carefree, and enthusiastic campers stayed to enjoy the picnic. (adjectives)

We searched under the desk, behind the shelves, in the trash can, and in the refrigerator for the missing keys. (prepositional phrases)

The series may be a listing of nouns, verbs, prepositional phrases, adjective clauses, or any other grammar structure, but they must all be the same structure.

Notice that there is a comma separating the last two items in each series. This comma is called a **serial comma** (or sometimes the "Oxford comma"), and it is important in ensuring that your series of items makes sense. Look at these examples:

My favorite foods are cheese, pizza and ice cream. (Pizza and ice cream together? No thanks!)

My favorite foods are cheese, pizza, and ice cream. (That's more like it—an appetizer, main course, and dessert.)

Note: If all of the items are separated by **and** or **or**, don't use commas to separate them at all.

Examples: I like to eat cheese and pizza and ice cream.

I should eat cheese or pizza or ice cream and not all three at the same meal.

When you're writing a sentence containing a series of items, make sure that the sentence uses parallel structure. That means that your series needs to be a list of grammatical equals. Look at the following examples:

Examples: A good bedtime routine is a hot shower, flossing and brushing your teeth, and to get your clothes ready for the next morning.

This sentence makes sense, but it's not parallel because the actions in the list are not in the same grammatical form. "A hot shower" is a noun with its modifiers. "Flossing and brushing your teeth" is a gerund phrase. "To get your clothes ready for the next morning" is an infinitive phrase. To improve the sentence so that it flows better, they should all be the same form. Here is the same sentence rewritten so that all the items are gerund phrases:

A good bedtime routine is taking a hot shower, flossing and brushing your teeth, and getting your clothes ready for the next morning.

Now you try: revise the sentence so that all of the list items are infinitive phrases:

A good bedtime routine is to take a hot shower, to floss and brush your teeth, and to get your clothes ready for the next morning.

Comma Rule 2: Two Adjectives Tests

Sometimes you use a comma to separate two or more adjectives preceding a noun. The reason this isn't a hard and fast rule is that we have expressions in English that we use together so often that they are seen as one unit, so to divide them with a comma would seem strange. There are a couple of tests you can use to check whether you need a comma or not.

And Test

The *and* test works like this: If it sounds natural to put *and* between the adjectives, use a comma. If *and* sounds awkward, leave it out.

Order Test

For this test, try changing the order of the adjectives. If you can change the order and the phrase still sounds okay and makes sense, you need commas between them. If you can't, leave them out.

Let's test a couple of sentences. Look at these examples:

1) I saw a little old man.

Do we need a comma? Let's test it.
And test: I saw a little *and* old man.
Order test: I saw an old little man.

This sounds strange to native English speakers because of the unwritten order that exists for adjectives. Leave out the comma.

Here's another sentence to test:

2) That is a narrow dangerous road.

And test: That is a narrow *and* dangerous road.
Order test: That is a dangerous narrow road.
Sounds great! This sentence needs a comma between *narrow* and *dangerous*:

This is a narrow, dangerous road.

You won't always have to use both tests to determine whether you need a comma, but you might want to if you're still not sure after the first one.

Why does it sound strange, though?

The reason we can't change the order of some adjectives without making the sentence sound strange to native English speakers is that there is a certain order for categories of adjectives. It's not anything we officially learn or memorize, but we know it. We use this order without even thinking about it! The categories are:

1) quantity	**4)** age	**7)** origin
2) opinion	**5)** color	**8)** material
3) size	**6)** shape	**9)** purpose

Adjectives from the same category can be rearranged, and they need commas between them. Adjectives from different categories, however, can't be rearranged. They need to be in this order or they sound strange to native English speakers—even if we don't know why!

Look back at our example sentence

> I saw a *little old man*.
> The adjectives are *little* and *old*.
> *little* = size
> *old* = age

Size comes before age on the list, so these adjectives are in the "right" order and they don't need commas. They can't be rearranged because then they wouldn't follow the order. That's why *old little man* sounds odd to us!

Don't worry, you don't have to memorize this list. This is just one of those interesting "grammar rules" that you already know, but you don't know that you know it! Isn't English cool?

Comma Rule 3: Compound Sentence

Use a comma before the conjunction joining independent clauses or sentences.

> **Example:** Brian changed the oil in the old Chevy, and Joe checked the spark plugs in the Pontiac.

There is a complete, stand-alone sentence on either side of the conjunction *and*, so you need a comma.

> **Example:** Brian changed the oil in the old Chevy and checked the spark plugs in the Pontiac.

There is not a complete, stand-alone sentence after the conjunction *and*. You do not need a comma here. It's simply a compound verb—*changed...and checked...*—with the same subject (*Brian*).

Exception to Comma Rule 3!

- If you are using the conjunction ***and,***

  AND

- either of the sentences contains <u>four words or fewer,</u>

  DON'T USE A COMMA.

> **Example:** Brian changed the oil and Joe checked the spark plugs on the Pontiac.

- The conjunction is ***and.***

- The first independent clause, *Brian changed the oil*, contains <u>only four words.</u>

This sentence meets both requirements for the exception, so no comma is needed here.

If you are using any other conjunction besides *and* in a compound sentence, you must use a comma.

Comma Rule 1: Exercise A

Directions

Apply Comma Rule 1 to these sentences and insert commas where they are needed. If the sentence is correct as written, write *correct* below it."Look at the lesson notes if you need help.

1) We had lessons in swimming, canoeing, archery, and handicrafts.

2) Mary and Frances and Ted dashed out of the car, down the beach, and into the water.

3) Our school has organized clubs for music, art, radio, and computers.

4) The high school orchestra includes violins, cellos, clarinets, saxophones, trumpets, and drums.

5) I've planted seedlings, fertilized them carefully, and watered them daily.

6) The children played happily on the swings, on the slide, and in the pool.

7) Science and Latin and algebra are all included in next year's curriculum.
   This sentence is correct because the nouns in the list are all separated by and.

8) Do you know how to put up a tent, to build a campfire, or to cook outdoors?

9) I enjoy swimming, boating, and surfing more than skiing, sledding, or skating.

10) Find out who is going to the picnic, what we must take, and when we should be there.

11) This morning Tom will wash the car, Zara will pack the lunch, and then we'll go for a drive.

12) In spite of bad predictions, the fog lifted, the sun shone, and everyone was happy.

13) Science teaches us how to conserve our forests, prevent erosion of the soil, and control our water supplies.

14) I would like to visit England, France, Spain, and Norway, the "Land of the Midnight Sun."

15) Soccer, basketball, and football are all strenuous sports.

Directions

Revise the following sentence so that it has a parallel structure.

16) The smell of cookies, going Christmas shopping, and how to keep a secret are all parts of what the holidays are about.

Answers will vary. Here are two possibilities:

Smelling cookies, going Christmas shopping, and keeping a secret are all parts of what the holidays are about.

To smell cookies, go Christmas shopping, and keep a secret are all part of what the holidays are about.

Directions

Each sentence below includes a comma split. Write the number that is beneath the comma split in the first space below the sentence. Write what the comma is splitting on the line next to the space.

Example: The happy, carefree, enthusiastic kids, enjoyed the picnic.
              1   2   3

     3   splits subject (kids) and verb (enjoyed)

17) The old, dog trotted slowly into the beautiful, elegant, immaculate house.
         1   2   3

     1   *splits modifier* (old) *and its noun* (dog)

18) The rain stopped, the sun came out, and the children continued their vigorous, strenuous, game.
            1   2   3   4

     4   *splits modifier* (strenuous) *and its noun* (game)

19) The gym teacher is carefully teaching, wrestling, gymnastics, and tumbling.
                    1   2   3

     1   *splits verb* (is teaching) *and direct object* (wrestling, gymnastics, and tumbling)

Comma Rule 2: Exercise B

Directions

Apply Comma Rule 2 to these sentences and insert commas where they are needed. If the sentence is correct as written, write ***correct*** below it. Look at the lesson notes if you need help.

1) John was the popular, efficient president of the senior class.

2) The cold, dry northern air is very invigorating.

3) We loved running barefoot over the damp, cool sand.

4) What a stern, dignified manner that soldier has!

5) The dark, dingy, musty attic seemed spooky.

6) The noisy, carefree fans cheered when they saw the bright blue uniforms of the band.

7) Have you read about the strong, courageous man who climbed the sheer, icy slopes of Mt. Everest?

8) An alert, hard-working, businesslike leader is needed.

9) A dark, squat iron stove stood in the corner of the cabin.

10) Alfred Hitchcock fascinated us with his thrilling, blood-curdling films.

11) It was a bright, brisk, beautiful autumn day.

12) A little old man knocked at the door.
     correct

13) That was a long, hard, exhausting bike ride.

14) Jupiter is a large, mysterious planet.

15) Althea Gibson played a powerful, brilliant game.

Directions

Revise the following sentence so that it has a parallel structure.

16) I love to eat, playing with my kitten, and a good conversation with a friend.

Answers will vary. Here are two possibilities:

> *I love eating, playing with my kitten, and having a good conversation with a friend.*

> *I love to eat, play with my kitten, and have a good conversation with a friend.*

Directions

Each sentence below includes a comma split. Write the number that is beneath the comma split in the first space below the sentence. Write what the comma is splitting on the line next to the space.

17) That, is a good, long, tough hike!
     1   2   3

  1   *splits subject* (That) *and verb* (is)

18) The young, creative boys are working on a new, innovative, computer.
         1   2   3

  3   *splits modifier* (innovative) *and its noun* (computer)

19) The dark, wet, musty tank smelled, terrible.
      1 2   3

  3   *splits linking verb* (smelled) *and predicate adjective* (terrible)

Comma Rule 3: Exercise C

Directions

Apply Comma Rule 3 to these sentences and insert commas where they are needed. Not all of the sentences may need a comma! If the sentence is correct as written, write **_correct_** below it. Look at the lesson notes if you need help.

1) There are many beautiful beaches along the coast, but one must get used to the cold water.

2) Henry came over, but Tom stayed at home.

3) I used red food coloring to make the hummingbird food, but my friend said that is not healthy for them.

4) Astronomy is an old science, yet it is now one of the most exciting.

5) Our teacher is using videos and apps in our Social Studies class, and we are really enjoying them.

6) She tried on eight pairs of shoes, but didn't buy any of them!
    correct

7) A robin has a nest in a tree near our porch, and we watch her feeding her babies.

8) Harry lived on a farm and had to get up early in the morning to do chores.
    correct

9) I will explain my theory once more, but you must listen.

10) The teacher explained the project and we went to work.
    correct

11) I'd love to go to the movies, but I have too much work to do.

12) The movie was excellent, but I didn't enjoy waiting in line.

13) We stopped on the side of the road and ate our lunch.
    correct

14) On the moon, the temperature rises to over 200 degrees in the daytime but drops far below zero at night.
    correct

15) There was an annoying noise in the car, but we could not locate the cause.

16) The coach drew a diagram and the players studied it.
    correct

Directions

Revise the following sentence so that it has a parallel structure.

17) A car that is poorly maintained, operating it beyond the speed limit, and to drink and drive can all be very dangerous.

Answers will vary. Two possible correct solutions are:

> *To maintain a car poorly, operate it beyond the speed limit, and drive while drinking can all be very dangerous.*

> *Maintaining a car poorly, operating it beyond the speed limit, and driving while drinking can all be very dangerous.*

Directions

Each sentence below includes a comma split. Write the number that is beneath the comma split in the first space below the sentence. Write what the comma is splitting on the line next to the space.

18) The girl in the blue dress, talked too fast, but she told fascinating, interesting stories.
              1   2   3

_1_   *splits subject* (girl) *and verb* (talked)

19) I craved a hot, delicious, cheesy pizza and drove in the pouring rain, ten miles.
              1   2   3

_3_   *splits verb* (drove) *and direct object* (miles)

20) My mother gave the girl who was just learning how to cook, the orders, but I followed them.
                                                              1   2

_1_   *splits indirect object* (girl) *and direct object* (orders)

Application & Enrichment

Paraphrasing: One Sentence Summaries

Directions

First, mark all of the nouns (***n***), proper nouns (***pn***), adjectives (***adj***), articles (***art***), pronouns (***pro***), and prepositions (***pp***) in the paragraph below. Put parentheses around the prepositional phrases.

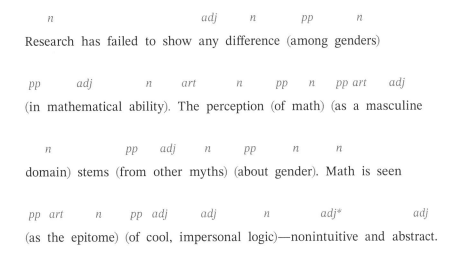

Next, paraphrase the passage. For this paraphrase, write a one-sentence summary of the main ideas in the passage. A **summary** is a short statement that provides only the main points. To write a summary sentence, there are a few simple things to remember:

- **Read the whole passage.** Unlike the previous exercise in which you were asked to paraphrase each individual sentence, you're being asked to **summarize the passage** in one sentence. That means that you will need to know what it says! Read it as many times as needed to be sure that you completely understand.

- **Identify the main idea (or ideas, in a longer passage).** Look for the nouns and verbs. Consider what modifiers are used to describe these parts of speech. Underline or circle the most important idea or ideas, if that helps.

- **Use your own words.** A one–sentence summary usually doesn't have enough room to quote from a passage. You also don't want to plagiarize the original passage!

- **Don't give your own opinion.** A summary is not the proper place to give your own thoughts on the subject. Simply restate the main idea(s) in your own words.

Directions

Write your answers to the following questions before writing your one-sentence summary.

Answers will vary. Possible answers are given.

1) In your opinion, what are the three most important nouns in this passage?

Answers will probably include three of the following: math, gender, ability, myth, logic.

Now think about how these nouns relate to each other. What verbs are used with them? What adjectives are used to modify them?

2) List one word or phrase from the passage that explains more about each of the three important nouns you chose in step 1. You can change the word or phrase slightly to say what you mean if the exact word you need is not in the passage, as long as your word choice doesn't show an opinion about the passage.

noun	explaining word or phrase
math	*logic*
gender	*masculine*
ability	*no difference*

3) Using the important words you identified as a guideline, what is the one main idea of the passage? Remember that the summary should be in your own words; however, it's okay if the unique sentence you write uses some of the words from the passage that you identified as important.

Math ability is not related to gender, in spite of stereotypes.

*These two adjectives are not in their usual place. If your student does not identify these as adjectives, explain to them that they are describing the noun "logic" even though they follow the noun. The job that a part of speech is doing can't always be determined by its position! We will discuss other locations where adjectives can be found in future lessons. For now, discuss with your student why they think the writer may have chosen to take these adjectives out of their normal order. Ask them which of these sentences is more dramatic and why:

"We stared at the dark and deep ocean."

"We stared at the ocean, dark and deep."

Comma Rules 1, 2, and 3: Assessment

Comma Rule 1—Items in a Series

Directions

Apply Comma Rule 1 and insert commas where they are needed. If the sentence is correct as written, write **correct** below it. Look at the lesson notes if you need help.

Each correctly placed comma is worth one point. It is also worth one point if your student correctly identifies that a sentence does not need any commas.

1) Students, teachers, parents, and visitors attended the picnic.

3

2) They roamed over the hills, through the fields, down to the lake, and across the bridge.

3

3) I bought a suit and a tie and a dress shirt yesterday.

1   *correct*

4) George Washington Carver derived from the peanut such items as ink, coffee, beauty

3   products, and pigments.

5) Do you want French or ranch or vinaigrette dressing on your salad?

1   *correct*

6) Mosquitoes buzzed, crickets chirped, and mockingbirds sang.

2

7) Robert Browning said that youth is good, that middle age is better, and that old

2   age is best.

8) Those who had walked to the picnic, who had brought small children, who had no

3   umbrella, or who had worn good clothes dashed to a nearby farmhouse.

9) The smell of hot dogs, the crack of a bat, and the cloudless summer sky always remind

2   me of the ballpark.

10) I borrowed *Holes*, *The Hobbit*, and *The Book Thief* from the library.

2

22

Comma Rule 2—Two Adjectives Tests

Directions

Apply Comma Rule 2 and insert commas where they are needed. If the sentence is correct as written, write **correct** below it. Look at the lesson notes if you need help.

Each correctly placed comma is worth one point. It is also worth one point if your student correctly identifies that a sentence does not need any commas.

_____ **11)** My aunt is a kind, generous, warm-hearted person.

    2

_____ **12)** We need the help of three strong people.

    1   *correct*

_____ **13)** A vain, talkative DJ annoys me.

    1

_____ **14)** Anna fluttered her gorgeous black eyelashes.

    1   *correct*

_____ **15)** We chose a beautiful mahogany end table.

    1   *correct*

_____ **16)** Round, deep craters and steep, rugged mountains dot the surface of the moon.

    2

_____ **17)** We passed the warm, humid afternoon playing Monopoly.

    1

_____ **18)** What a wide, smooth highway this is!

    1

_____ **19)** If one is not in a hurry, the quaint little stores of old Alexandria are very inviting.

    1

_____ **20)** The crowded, uncomfortable dining car was no pleasure for anyone.

    1

    ‾‾

    12

Comma Rule 3—Compound Sentence

Directions

Apply Comma Rule 3 and insert commas where they are needed. If the sentence is correct as written, write correct below it. Look at the lesson notes if you need help.

Each correctly placed comma is worth one point. It is also worth one point if your student correctly identifies that a sentence does not need any commas.

_____ **21)** Everyone was at the game, but Quincy arrived an hour late.
1

_____ **22)** Either the gift was lost in the mail, or he had forgotten to thank me.
1

_____ **23)** Into the garbage can she flung the burned cake and immediately started work on another.
1   *correct*

_____ **24)** The critics hated the play, but it ran for six months.
1

_____ **25)** Ethan whispered something to Juan and quickly left the stadium.
1   *correct*

_____ **26)** Maya picked the flowers and Jan arranged them.
1

_____ **27)** Beaumont led in the first inning by two runs, but Houston took the lead in the second.
1

_____ **28)** Rescue workers helped farmers to clear away debris and replant their ruined crops after
1   the flood.

_____ **29)** The *Titanic* was considered an unsinkable ship, but she sank in the North Atlantic on
1   April 14, 1912.

_____ **30)** At last, the weather became more merciful and settled down to normal.
1

_____
10

Comma Rules 1–3

Directions

Use the three comma rules you have learned so far and insert commas where they are needed. If the sentence is correct as written, write correct below it. Look at the lesson notes if you need help.

Each correctly placed comma is worth one point. It is also worth one point if your student correctly identifies that a sentence does not need any commas.

_____ **31)** A beach party was planned for Saturday, but the weather looked bad.
1

_____ **32)** We invited John, Maya, Jen, and Adam.
3

_____ **33)** Mom helped us with the refreshments and Adam brought some games.
1   *correct*

_____ **34)** We ate pizza, played Trivial Pursuit, and watched a funny old beach-blanket movie.
2

_____ **35)** It was actually a fun, lazy, relaxing afternoon.
2

_____ **36)** Maya said she was bored and tried to organize a game of soccer.
1   *correct*

_____ **37)** Before we could play, we had to look all over the house to find the soccer ball, find
2   jackets, and find some shoes for John.

_____ **38)** After the soccer game, Jen stretched out on the couch and took a blissful snooze.
1

_____ **39)** We waited until she was fast asleep and then drew a mustache on her upper lip.
1   *correct*

_____ **40)** Jen woke up, saw the mustache, and took off after us!
2

═══
16

Non-Parallel Sentences

Directions

Revise the following sentences to make them parallel.

Answers will vary. Two possible solutions are provided for each sentence.

_____ **41)** To learn some new words, writing a good essay, and how to analyze our language are
5   major parts of our English teacher's curriculum.

> *Learning some new words, writing a good essay, and analyzing our language are ...*

> *To learn some new words, write a good essay, and analyze our language are ...*

_____ **42)** My hometown has all the advantages: the weather is good, friendly neighbors, with
5   excellent schools, and fine shopping.

> *My hometown has all the advantages: good weather, friendly neighbors, excellent schools, and fine shopping.*

> *My hometown has all the advantages: the weather is good, the neighbors are friendly, the schools are excellent, and the shopping is fine.*

10

Comma Splits

Directions

There is a comma split in each sentence below. Write the number that is under the comma split in the first space below the sentence. Then write what the comma is splitting on the line next to the number.

Give two points for correctly identifying the comma split and one point for correctly writing what the comma is splitting, for a total of three possible points.

___2___ **43)** The man who lives next door, wants his children to excel in school, but he fails to give them
                                         1   2

careful, consistent help.
           3

___1___   *splits subject* (man) *and verb* (wants)

___2___ **44)** The student in this class are reading in the spring semester, a wonderful book which
                                                                    1

contains adventure, fantasy, and romance.
                    2   3

___1___   *splits verb* (are reading) *and direct object* (book)

___2___ **45)** The frigid, icy air made it difficult for people to breathe, but coach kept us out to practice for
                            1   2

our upcoming, match against South High.
                 3

___3___   *splits modifier* (upcoming) *and its noun* (match)

===
6

=== *Total Points* $\dfrac{61}{76} = 80\%$
76

Comma Rule 4

Lesson 3: Comma Rule 4: Nonessential Modifiers

Comma Rule 4

Use a comma to separate nonessential adjective clauses and nonessential participial phrases from the rest of the sentence. Remember: Adjective clauses and participial phrases are groups of words that act like adjectives. They modify nouns and pronouns.

Example 1: My English teacher, who loves books, reads all the time.

The group of words *who loves books* describes the noun *teacher*. You will notice that the noun being modified is almost always directly before the clause or phrase that modifies it.

Let's review how to identify a participial phrase and an adjective clause, since we first learned about them in the previous level:*

A **participial phrase** begins with either a **present participle** (a verb ending in -ing) or a **past participle** (a verb that fits in the sentence *"I have _____."*).

Examples 2: Pumpkin, *sleeping in the window,* is purring happily.

Her hammock, *received as a gift,* is her favorite place to nap.

An **adjective clause** almost always begins with a relative pronoun *(who, whose, whom, which, and that).*

Example 3: Pumpkin, *who is a very happy cat,* has an extremely loud purr.

*Refer to your notes from Level 4 for more info on identifying participial phrases and adjective clauses.

Once you have located a participial phrase or adjective clause, you need to decide whether it is **essential** or **nonessential** to the sentence. If you remove the entire phrase or clause, can the reader still understand what the sentence is really saying?

Example 4: Jim Riley, *who skips school repeatedly,* is not doing well in his classes.

If we remove the adjective clause *who skips school repeatedly,* we're left with *Jim Riley is not doing well in his classes.* Even without the adjective clause, we know who is not doing well in their classes. The adjective clause is **nonessential**. That's why it has commas around it—the commas set it apart from the rest of the sentence.

Important: If the nonessential modifier is in the beginning or end of a sentence, you only need one comma to set it apart. However, if it's in the middle of a sentence, make sure you use two commas— one at the beginning and one at the end of the phrase or clause—so you don't accidentally create a comma split!

Example 5: Students *who skip school repeatedly* do not often do well in their classes.

In this case, if we remove the adjective clause *who skip school repeatedly,* we are left with a sentence that doesn't communicate what we are trying to say: *Students do not often do well in their classes.* It does not have commas around it because it is **essential** to the reader's understanding.

Here's a trick: One way to help you determine whether a clause or phrase is essential or not is to read the sentence with as much expression as you can. Pretend you're a TV news announcer and really be dramatic—have fun! If the modifier is **nonessential**, you will have a natural tendency to pause right where the commas go. If it's **essential**, there will be no tendency to pause. This trick doesn't always work, but you can use it to help you make the decision!

Comma Rule 4: Exercise A

Directions

Underline the adjective clause or participial phrase in each sentence. After each sentence, write *AC* if it's an adjective clause or *part* if it's a participial phrase. Separate all **nonessential** phrases or clauses from the rest of the sentence with commas. Remember that some phrases or clauses are essential to the sentence! Look at your lesson notes if you need help.

1) Senator Stewart, hoping for a compromise, began an impassioned speech.

    part

2) I bought all the books written by John Grisham at a garage sale.

    part

3) The Foresman Building, which has become a firetrap, will be torn down.

    AC

4) Sometimes I feel like throwing all the clothes that are in my closet into the trash!

    AC

5) Students who watch television until early in the morning may not do their best the next day.

    AC

6) My grandfather Ben, sitting in his favorite chair, would always tell us stories before bedtime.

    part

7) Give this note to the girl sitting on the sofa.

    part

8) The senior representative from Zambia, dressed in his native costume, made a colorful sight.

    part

9) The kids who sing in the choir enjoy performing for the other students.

    AC

10) The candidate of my choice, kissing babies like a seasoned campaigner, was learning about politics quickly.

    part

Directions

In each sentence below there is a comma split. All of the commas in each sentence and the lines below them are numbered. Identify the comma split and write its number in the space next to the sentence number. On the lines under each, write what the comma is splitting on the appropriate line. For the correctly placed commas, write the comma rule "buzzword" on the numbered line.

Example: <u>1</u>   Students who skip school repeatedly, will be expelled, but our enthusiatic, dedicated

                                                     1   2   3

        students never skip.

#1 <u>splits subject (students) and verb (will be expelled)</u>

#2 <u>compound sentence</u>

#3 <u>two adjectives tests</u>

<u> 3 </u> **11)** John Wilson, elected by a large majority, began planning, a huge victory celebration.

              1   2   3

#1 *nonessential modifiers*

#2 *nonessential modifiers*

#3 *splits verb (planning) and direct object (celebration)*

<u> 1 </u> **12)** We have, soft, luxurious carpet in our living room, dining room, and hall.

              1   2   3   4

#1 *splits verb (have) and direct object (carpet)*

#2 *two adjectives tests*

#3 *items in a series*

#4 *items in a series*

<u> 1 </u> **13)** Students, who have a lot of homework should budget their time, but often they waste

                    1   2

        their energy in useless, futile procrastination.

                       3

#1 *splits subject (students) and verb (should budget)*

#2 *compound sentence*

#3 *two adjectives test*

Comma Rule 4: Exercise B

Directions

Underline the adjective clause or participial phrase in each sentence. After each sentence, write **AC** if it's an adjective clause or ***part*** if it's a participial phrase. Separate all **nonessential** phrases or clauses from the rest of the sentence with commas. Remember that some phrases or clauses are essential to the sentence! Look at your lesson notes if you need help. One sentence has two modifiers, so be sure to find both!

1) The pitcher, thinking the runner was out, started walking off the field.

   part

2) Here is my cousin Jamie, whom you met yesterday.

   AC

3) Maria, who enjoys her class in physics, will be an excellent engineer

   AC

4) Louis Pasteur, striving to save a little boy from death by rabies, developed a vaccine which finally conquered that dreadful disease.

   part, AC

5) The people who discovered radium were Marie and Pierre Curie.

   AC

6) E.T. Seton, who was a famous artist-naturalist, was born in England in 1860.

   AC

7) *Wild Animals I Have Known*, which is one of his most popular works, was his first book.

   AC

8) Kids who enjoy reading often do well in school.

   AC

9) The boy playing left end is our best tackle.

   part

10) The winning runners, breathing hard and visibly tired, broke the tape at the same time.

   part

11) Lake Superior, <u>covering an area of 30,000 square miles</u>, is the largest Great Lake.

part

12) The girl <u>working next to you</u> is my sister.

part

13) The students, <u>having gorged themselves on junk food</u>, called the picnic a huge success.

part

14) My turquoise and silver ring, <u>which we bought in Mexico</u>, is my favorite.

AC

15) A meal <u>cooked by my dad</u> is always a treat.

part

16) Only the students <u>gathered in the auditorium</u> got to hear the guest speaker.

part

17) John, <u>studying for the history exam</u>, was glad he had kept up with his reading.

part

18) My parents always loved the gifts <u>that I made myself</u>.

AC

19) Our new school library, <u>which has just been opened</u>, is a great asset to our school.

AC

20) The cat took a snooze in the warm sunlight <u>streaming through the living room window</u>.

part

Directions

In each sentence below there is a comma split. All of the commas in each sentence and the lines below them are numbered. Identify the comma split and write its number in the space next to the sentence number. On the lines under each, write what the comma is splitting on the appropriate line. For the correctly placed commas, write the comma rule "buzzword" on the numbered line.

_2_ **21)** I have a huge, overpowering urge to tell that nice person that their indescribable, kindness
1   2

has made my day, which was not going well until now.
3

#1 _two adjectives tests_

#2 _splits modifier (indescribable) and its noun (kindness)_

#3 _nonessential modifier_

_1_ **22)** I was reading, a really thrilling, mysterious book, but my mom, my dad, and my big sister
1   2   3   4   5

told me how it ends!

#1 _splits verb (was reading) and direct object (book)_

#2 _two adjectives tests_

#3 _compound sentence_

#4 _items in a series_

#5 _items in a series_

_1_ **23)** The kids in the band, decided to raise money, and their idea was to have a
1   2

dance, a bake sale, and a car wash.
3   4

#1 _splits subject (kids) and verb (decided)_

#2 _compound sentence_

#3 _items in a series_

#4 _items in a series_

Comma Rule 4: Exercise C

Directions

Apply Comma Rule 4 to the following sentences and insert commas where they are needed. Circle the word that the participial phrase or adjective clause modifies. One sentence has two modifiers, so be sure to find both!

1) (Ruth Snyder,) who is my second cousin, will visit me next summer.

2) We get the (Shreveport Times,) which is an excellent newspaper.

3) All (highways) that have eight lanes are near big cities.

4) You're a lot like my (dad,) who loves to tinker with old cars.

5) I think (people) who dye their hair unusual colors are very brave!

6) (Hepzibah Humperdinck,) who goes by the name Heppy, is my neighbor.

7) I attend (Cranford High School,) which has an enrollment of 598.

8) All (contestants) answering this question correctly will win a prize.

9) The hog-nosed (snake,) feared by many, is not poisonous.

10) In (The Hobbit,) which is a very exciting book, (Bilbo,) who is extremely excitable, becomes adventurous and unafraid.

Directions

Write four sentences, using the adjective clauses or participial phrase provided.

Answers will vary.

11) Use *who passed this grammar unit* as a **nonessential** modifier.

Jim Smith, who passed this grammar unit, is learning to be a good writer.

12) Use *who passed this grammar unit* as an **essential** modifier.

Students who passed this grammar unit are learning how to use commas.

13) Use *running in the house* as a **nonessential** modifier.

My little brother, running in the house, knocked over the end table.

14) Use *running in the house* as an **essential** modifier.

My mom sent kids running in the house outside to play.

Directions

Write four sentences of your own demonstrating the following comma rules. Have fun and be creative!

Answers will vary.

15) Use **Comma Rule 1, Items in a Series,** in a sentence:

16) Use **Comma Rule 2, Two Adjectives Tests,** in a sentence:

17) Use **Comma Rule 3, Compound Sentence,** in a sentence:

18) Use **Comma Rule 4, Nonessential Modifier,** in a sentence:

Directions

In each sentence below there is a comma split. All of the commas in each sentence and the spaces below them are numbered. Identify the comma split and write its number in the space next to the sentence number. In the space under each, write what it is splitting on the appropriate line. For the correctly placed commas, write the comma rule "buzzword" in the numbered space.

_2_ **19)** The delicious, succulent turkey that was cooked by Chef Andre, won first prize, but
                          1   2   3

Georgine's souffle won second prize.

#1 *two adjectives tests*

#2 *splits subject* (turkey) *and verb* (won)

#3 *compound sentence*

_1_ **20)** The woman in the store looked, incredibly angry at the poor clerk, who was trying
                                1   2

desperately to wrap an awkward, bulky package.
                                3

#1 *splits linking verb* (looked) *and predicate adjective* (angry)

#2 *nonessential modifiers*

#3 *two adjectives test*

_3_ **21)** Bruce Willis, Denzel Washington, and Julia Roberts, were big stars in the 1990s.
                1   2   3

#1 *items in a series*

#2 *items in a series*

#3 *splits subject* (Bruce Willis, Denzel Washington, and Julia Roberts)

       and verb (were)

Application & Enrichment
Online Spelling and Grammar Checkers

In your career as a writer, whether at school or in the workplace, you will probably use some kind of online word processing program that includes a spelling checker and maybe even a grammar checker. Great! That makes your life so much easier—less to think about, right?

Knot rilly. Eye em shore ewe have scene thinks wear their are spilling mistakes.

Translation: *Not really. I am sure you have seen things where there are spelling mistakes.*

There is a reason for that: spell check isn't helpful if the error you make is still a word. All of the words in our garbled sentence are still words—it's just that many of them are not the right word for the sentence! A computer program might know that, but it might not. If you allow spell check or grammar check to do all of your proofreading, you could be risking a word choice or spelling error.

Grammar checkers can be useful in finding missing punctuation or awkward sentence structure, but their suggestions are not always useful. Consider the following sentence. This is a common example of a sentence constructed in Pennsylvania Dutch, a local dialect spoken near the Analytical Grammar home office, and its diagram:

Throw the horse over the fence some hay.

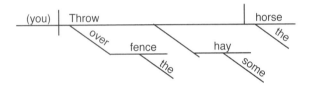

Let's see. *Throw* is clearly the verb here. With the misplaced modifier *over the fence*, however, it makes a pretty crazy sentence, because it looks like it's the horse that's being thrown! That poor horse! *Some hay* could be an indirect object, perhaps, although that's really unclear from the construction of the sentence.

The good news is that a couple of different grammar checkers had a question about this sentence, too. The bad news is that the only suggestion they made is to add a conjunction:

Throw the horse over the fence and some hay.

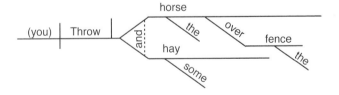

Now we have a compound direct object: *horse* and *hay*. So the poor horse is still going over the fence, but at least his dinner is being flung after him.

Or possibly, we are throwing him over the fence and partway through the field of hay on the other side of it:

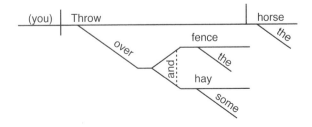

The grammar checker's suggestion was no help in fixing our sentence at all, and, had we just clicked "accept," we would still be left with a nonsensical sentence.

Enough silliness. What is this sentence really saying? The horse is on the other side of the fence. Throw the hay over to him. So the proper, grammatically correct way to write the sentence is:

Throw the horse some hay over the fence.

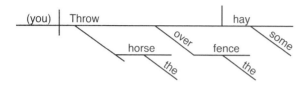

Horse is the indirect object; *hay* is the direct object. *Over the fence* is an adverbial prepositional phrase modifying *Throw*. This sentence construction not only makes grammatical sense but also logical sense. But the online grammar checkers didn't know that, because they can't (quite) think like a human yet.

Grammar and spelling checkers can be useful tools in flagging questionable material, but they can't take the place of the human brain. When suggestions are made, review each one carefully. Because you are completing this program, you have the instincts and tools to make sure that you end up with the finished product you intend. Look at each suggestion, but trust yourself and learn how to use the "ignore" button!

Directions

Circle the word or words that are incorrect in each sentence. Replace the wrong (but correctly spelled) word with the correct word. You will need to carefully read for context.

1) I asked him if he had (scene) the movie yet.

seen

2) The quarterback (through) the (bawl) forty yards down the field for a catch!

threw, ball

3) The elegant (wring) included a diamond (waying) three (carrots.)

ring, weighing, carats

4) Science has proven that cats (per) at a (heeling) frequency.

purr, healing

5) I was starving, so I (eight) four slices of pizza last (knight) after practice.

ate, night

Directions

Rewrite the following grammatically incorrect sentences to make logical sense. If they are correct, write "ignore." Parse or diagram the sentence if it helps.

Answers will vary. One possible solution is provided.

6) My father the dinner bill paid.

My father paid the dinner bill.

7) No longer keeping things cold, we replaced the refrigerator.

We replaced the refrigerator that was no longer keeping things cold.

8) Across the park, the dog chased the squirrel wildly.

ignore or The dog chased the squirrel wildly across the park.

9) Will you into the hamper put your laundry?

Will you put your laundry into the hamper?

10) Extremely dependent on internet access, a wifi outage makes my household chaos.

My household, extremely dependent on internet access, becomes chaos with a wifi outage.

Comma Rule 4: Assessment

Directions

Underline all participial phrases and adjective clauses in the following sentences. Circle the noun or pronoun that each phrase or clause modifies. Insert commas where they are needed, using Comma Rule 4.

The following are worth one point each:

- *Identifying the participial phrase/adjective clause*
- *Identifying the noun or pronoun being modified by the phrase/clause*
- *Properly placing each necessary comma*
- *Leaving out commas in sentences where they are not needed*

Example: My (brother,) who is an excellent basketball player, got a scholarship to Temple.

___ **1)** In my grandparents' day, teenagers liked to single out a (hero) who could sing or act.
3

___ **2)** This hero (worship,) which our grandparents said was a common affliction of
4   teenagers, took many forms.

___ **3)** When Elvis crooned and swiveled his way through a song, his (audience,) reacting
4   hysterically to his singing, screamed or even fainted!

___ **4)** During his (reign,) which lasted longer than the older generation expected, his
4   followers imitated his hairstyle and ways of speaking and moving.

___ **5)** Then the (Beatles,) blasting onto the scene in the early 60's, stole much of the
7   limelight from (Elvis,) who didn't have a cute British accent or choirboy haircut.

___ **6)** Beatles (posters,) which were a necessity to every fan, were soon pushing Elvis items
4   off the shelves.

___ **7)** Every young (man) who wanted to be "cool" had a Beatles haircut.
3

___ **8)** Even the mighty Beatles eventually had to make way for (those) who were now
3   taking the music-buying public by storm.

_____ **9)** Elvis and the Beatles were two of the first (artists) in the rock-n-roll age <u>that took</u>
  3   <u>the new market of teenagers by storm.</u>

_____ **10)** Before this time, (teenagers) <u>interested in music</u> were likely to listen to the same
  3   music as their parents.

=====
  38

Directions

Using Comma Rule 4, insert commas where they are needed. Write **correct** underneath the sentence if there are no errors.

Each properly placed comma is worth one point. Identifying a sentence where a comma is not needed is worth one point.

____ **11)** All students planning to attend the student council meeting are excused at 2:00.
1   *correct*

____ **12)** Louis Pasteur, working in his laboratory, took time out to treat people for rabies.
2

____ **13)** The fifty-story Civic Center, located on the corner of Main and Daniels, was
2   evacuated this afternoon due to a small fire in the lobby.

____ **14)** Every child enrolling in school for the first time must be accompanied by a parent
1   or guardian.
            correct

____ **15)** Their youngest daughter, loved by everyone, is not at all spoiled.
2

____ **16)** Anyone seeing a suspicious person should notify the police immediately.
1   *correct*

____ **17)** A surprise phone call wishing you happy birthday is a nice gift.
1   *correct*

____ **18)** My left index finger, badly bruised by the blow, began to swell.
2

____ **19)** Miss Danby, trying not to laugh, offered to help us with the stage makeup.
2

____ **20)** The House of Tiles, built in Mexico City in the sixteenth century, is now known
2   as Sanborn's.

____
16

Directions

In each sentence below, there is a comma split. All of the commas in each sentence and the spaces below them are numbered. Identify the comma split and write its number in the space next to the sentence number. In the space under each, write what it is splitting on the appropriate line. For the correctly placed commas, write the comma rule "buzzword" in the numbered space.

Correctly identifying the comma split is worth two points. Correctly identifying what is being split and appropriate comma rule buzzword is worth one point each.

_1_ / _2_ **21)** The All-Breed Dog Show this weekend, will begin at 9:00 on Friday morning,
1   2

10:00 on Saturday morning, and noon on Sunday.
3

#1 / _1_ *splits subject* (All-Breed Dog Show) *and verb* (will begin)

#2 / _1_ *items in a series*

#3 / _1_ *items in a series*

_2_ / _2_ **22)** The beautiful, elegant, model walked gracefully across the stage, but she stopped and
1   2   3

posed when she saw the camera.

#1 / _1_ *two adjectives tests*

#2 / _1_ *splits modifier* (elegant) *and noun* (model)

#3 / _1_ *compound sentence*

_3_ / _2_ **23)** The winning student, who made a terrific speech, told me, a very funny story about
1   2   3

how he prepared for it.

#1 / _1_ *nonessential modifier*

#2 / _1_ *nonessential modifier*

#3 / _1_ *splits indirect object* (me) *and direct object* (story)

___1___ **24)** I am definitely, a real fan of old movies, early 50s rock-and-roll, and vintage clothes.
2   1   2   3

___ **#1** *splits linking verb* (am) *and complement* (fan) _____
1

___ **#2** *items in a series* _____
1

___ **#3** *items in a series* _____
1

___3___ **25)** John, having seen Star Trek four times, doesn't want, to see it again, but I could see it
2   1   2   3   4

ten more times!

___ **#1** *nonessential modifier* _____
1

___ **#2** *nonessential modifier* _____
1

___ **#3** *splits verb* (does want) *and direct object* (to see it again) _____
1

___ **#4** *compound sentence* _____
1

═══
26

═══ *Total Points* $\dfrac{64}{80} = 80\%$
80

Comma Rule 5

Lesson 4: Comma Rule 5

To make our writing more engaging, we can use **introductory elements** to draw readers into the sentence. These elements are not essential to the understanding of the sentence, but they add extra information to provide context. Introductory elements are usually set apart from the rest of the sentence with a comma.

Comma Rule 5

Introductory element

An introductory element is a word, phrase, or clause at the beginning of a sentence that may add extra information but is not essential for understanding the sentence. These elements are usually set apart from the rest of the sentence with a comma.

The buzzword for this comma rule is **introductory element**. There are four different types of introductory elements to become familiar with:

A) Introductory interjection:

We have finally reached the ninth and final part of speech: the **interjection**! Interjections are words that express emotion: joy, wonder, anger, frustration, disgust, and so on. These words often come at the beginning of a sentence and serve no grammatical function in the sentence. They can be removed from the sentence without changing its meaning. Interjections are usually single words or sounds like *yes, well, no, why, oh,* or *ew,* but any word can act as an interjection. Sometimes an interjection has more than one word, like *my goodness* or *heavens to Betsy.*

Interjections are set apart from the rest of the sentence by a comma or an exclamation point—but since this lesson is about commas, we will only use commas for now.

Example: *Why*, you must be exhausted!

Why can be removed from the sentence without changing the meaning. It serves no grammatical function in the sentence.

B) Introductory participial phrase

Put a comma after an introductory participial phrase. Remember, a participle is a verb that either ends in *-ing* or fits into the sentence "*I have* _____."*

Example: *Pausing in the doorway*, the new student smiled timidly.

Pausing in the doorway tells us **why** *the new student smiled timidly*, but the sentence still makes sense if that phrase is removed. It is nonessential to the sentence.

*Refer to your notes on participial phrases from Level 4 if needed.

C) Introductory adverb clause

Put a comma after an introductory adverb clause. Remember the "thumb test" for finding out if a group of words is an adverb clause. Put your left thumb over the subordinating conjunction and your right thumb over the independent clause. If what you have left is a sentence, you know that the introductory group of words is an adverb clause. Try it with the sentence below: First, put your left thumb over the subordinating conjunction *After*. Next, put your right thumb over everything that follows the comma. Between your thumbs you have *Bill hit the ball*. That's a sentence, so you know that *After Bill hit the ball* is an adverb clause.*

Example: *After Bill hit the ball*, the crowd cheered.

After Bill hit the ball tells us **when** the crowd cheered, but the sentence still makes sense if the adverb clause is removed. It is nonessential to the sentence.

*Refer to your notes from Level 4 on adverb clauses and subordinating conjunctions if needed.

D) Introductory prepositional phrase

Put a comma after an introductory prepositional phrase. If there is more than one prepositional phrase at the beginning of the sentence, put a comma after the last one.

Example: (*Near the gate*)(at *the end of the corral*), the horse stood quietly.

There are two prepositional phrases at the beginning of this sentence: *Near the gate and at the end of the corral*. You don't need a comma between them, but put a comma after the second one to make it easier for the reader to understand.

Note: Some grammar programs teach that a comma is not necessary after one introductory prepositional phrase, as long as the sentence is not confusing without it. For example, which sentence below is easier to understand?

> In our state sales tax is rather rare.

> In our state, sales tax is rather rare.

In the first sentence, *state* could be modifying *sales tax*. That would make *sales tax* the object of the prepositional phrase *In our state sales tax* and leaves us with a sentence fragment without a subject. In the second sentence, with a comma after the short prepositional phrase *In our state*, it is clear that *sales tax* is the subject of the sentence. If you have any doubt about whether a sentence is unclear without the comma, go ahead and include it. Remember that punctuation's job is to guide your reader, so if using a comma will help them understand your sentence without having to reread it, it's best to put it in!

Comma Rule 5: Exercise A

Directions

Underline and identify the introductory element in each sentence, using the following abbreviations:

int = interjection

part = participial phrase

prep = prepositional phrase(s)

ac = adverb clause

Insert commas where they are needed.

1) Yes, Paula is my sister.

 int

2) Climbing down a tree, I ripped my pocket on a sharp twig.

 part

3) Since you collect coins, you might want this one.

 ac

4) While we were vacationing in Montreal, we met many French-speaking people.

 ac

5) In the morning, mail is delivered to our house.

 prep

6) When we entered, the room was empty.

 ac

7) In a corner of the garden, the dog had buried all of his bones.

 prep

8) While she was painting, my sister accidentally broke a window.

 ac

9) On the morning of the third day, the stranded hikers began to worry.

 prep

10) Say, do you know where the key to the clock is?

 int

Directions

In each sentence below, there is a comma split. All of the commas in each sentence and the lines below them are numbered. Identify the comma split and write its number in the space next to the sentence number. On the lines under each, write what the comma is splitting on the appropriate line. For the correctly placed commas, write the comma rule "buzzword" on the numbered line.

_1_ **11)** After Bill, hit the ball, the enthusiastic, exuberant crowd cheered, but the home team
　　　　　　　1　　　　　2　　　　　　　3　　　　　　　　　　4

lost anyway.

　#1 _splits subject_ (Bill) _and verb_ (hit)

　#2 _introductory elements_

　#3 _two adjectives tests_

　#4 _compound sentence_

_3_ **12)** John, who scored the top grade on the math final, has been given, the opportunity to
　　　　　1　　　　　　　　　　　　　　　　　　　　　　　2　　　　　3

attend a special math camp this summer.

　#1 _nonessential modifier_

　#2 _nonessential modifier_

　#3 _splits verb_ (has been given) _and direct object_ (opportunity)

_1_ **13)** Henry told Jill, a silly, ridiculous joke that really wasn't funny, but she
　　　　　　　　　1　　　2　　　　　　　　　　　　　　　　　3

laughed anyway.

　#1 _splits indirect object_ (Jill) _and direct object_ (joke)

　#2 _two adjectives tests_

　#3 _compound sentence_

Comma Rule 5: Exercise B

Directions

Underline and identify the introductory element in each sentence, using the following abbreviations:

int = interjection

part = participial phrase

prep = prepositional phrase(s)

ac = adverb clause

Insert commas where they are needed.

1) <u>Practiced in China thousands of years ago</u>, falconry is an ancient sport.

   part

2) <u>Like the hawk</u>, a falcon has a curved beak.

   prep

3) <u>Although falconry is an ancient sport</u>, many people still enjoy it today.

   ac

4) <u>Having sharp claws and hooked beaks</u>, falcons are naturally good hunters.

   part

5) <u>In the place of guns</u>, some sportsmen use falcons for hunting.

   prep

6) <u>After she has learned to fly</u>, a female falcon is taken from the nest and tamed.

   ac

7) <u>Until the falcon becomes accustomed to living around humans</u>, she wears a hood.

   ac

8) <u>Covering the eyes and head</u>, this leather hood helps the hunter control the bird.

   part

9) <u>While the falcon has the hood on</u>, the hunter carries the bird to the field.

   ac

10) <u>In the field</u>, the desired prey is located.

    prep

11) <u>When the hunter sees his prey and takes the hood off</u>, the falcon instinctively attacks.

    ac

12) <u>In addition to a hood</u>, other implements are used in falconry.

    prep

13) <u>During a hunt</u>, a falconer usually wears a heavy leather gauntlet or glove.

    prep

14) <u>When they are training a young falcon to hunt</u>, they also use lures.

    ac

15) <u>Used properly</u>, lures teach falcons to attack certain birds.

    part

16) <u>Containing pieces of meat and feathers</u>, the lure quickly attracts the falcon.

    part

17) <u>Within seconds</u>, a hungry falcon usually pounces upon the lure.

    prep

18) <u>Yes</u>, falcons become trained hunters in a short time.

    int

19) <u>Since the falcon's speed and accuracy are extremely effective</u>, guns are unnecessary.

    ac

20) <u>In a field with a falcon</u>, hunters often use dogs to retrieve the game.

    prep

Directions

In each sentence below there is a comma split. All of the commas in each sentence and the lines below them are numbered. Identify the comma split and write its number in the space next to the sentence number. On the lines under each, write what the comma is splitting on the appropriate line. For the correctly placed commas, write the comma rule "buzzword" on the numbered line.

_1_ **21)** Three students in Mrs. Finley's 3rd hour class have received, awards for
                                                                       1

attendance, courtesy, and academic excellence.
            2   3

#1 _splits verb_ (have recieved) _and direct object_ (awards)

#2 _items in a series_

#3 _items in a series_

_2_ **22)** The happy, excited, fans ran out onto the football field, and they carried the triumphant
                    1   2   3

coach around the track.

#1 _two adjectives tests_

#2 _splits modifier_ (excited) _and its noun_ (fans)

#3 _compound sentence_

_4_ **23)** In a drawer in my dresser, I keep my diary, which contains my innermost thoughts, but
                                      1   2   3

no one except me, is allowed to see it.
                  4

#1 _introductory element_

#2 _nonessential modifier_

#3 _nonessential modifier/compound sentence_ (either is correct)

#4 _splits subject_ (no one) _and verb_ (is allowed)

Comma Rule 5: Exercise C

Directions

Underline and identify the introductory element in each sentence, using the following abbreviations:

> **int** = interjection
>
> **part** = participial phrase
>
> **prep** = prepositional phrase(s)
>
> **ac** = adverb clause

Insert commas where they are needed.

1) <u>My goodness</u>, the entire story is false.
   int

2) <u>Washing and polishing the car for hours</u>, the boys found they were tired.
   part

3) <u>While Mario put the costume on</u>, the accompanist played "Rhapsody in Blue."
   ac

4) <u>At the edge of the deep woods near Lakeville in Cumberland County</u>, they built a small cabin.
   prep

5) <u>Among some cultures</u>, competition is unpopular.
   prep

6) <u>Oh</u>, I wouldn't be too sure of that.
   int

7) <u>Behaving like a spoiled child</u>, he sulked and pouted for hours.
   part

8) <u>When we had finished playing</u>, the piano was rolled offstage to make room for the next act.
   ac

9) <u>On the afternoon of the first day of school</u>, the halls are filled with confused 7th graders.
   prep

10) <u>Driven beyond her patience</u>, the teacher slammed her book on the desk.
    part

11) <u>In a minute</u>, I will leave for home.
    prep

12) <u>In the dark</u>, shadows can seem menacing.
    prep

Directions

Write sentences according to the following instructions. Be sure to use commas properly! Look back at your lesson notes if you need help.

Answers will vary.

13) A sentence with an introductory interjection

14) A sentence with an introductory participial phrase

15) A sentence with two or more introductory prepositional phrases

16) A sentence with an introductory adverb clause

17) A sentence including items in a series

18) A sentence demonstrating "two adjectives tests"

19) A compound sentence

20) A sentence including a nonessential modifier

Directions

In each sentence below there is a comma split. All of the commas in each sentence and the spaces below them are numbered. Identify the comma split and write its number in the space next to the sentence number. In the space under each, write what it is splitting on the appropriate line. For the correctly placed commas, write the comma rule "buzzword" in the numbered space.

_4_ **21)** Speaking on the intercom, Mr. Campbell, who is our principal, read us, the morning

                                  1   2   3   4

announcements in his clear voice.

#1 _introductory element_

#2 _nonessential modifier_

#3 _nonessential modifier_

#4 _splits indirect object_ (us) _and direct object_ (announcements)

_5_ **22)** Well, I have a particular reason, which I certainly don't want to explain, for not doing

         1   2   3

my complicated, confusing, homework!

                 4   5

#1 _introductory element_

#2 _nonessential modifier_

#3 _nonessential modifier_

#4 _two adjectives tests_

#5 _splits modifier_ (confusing) _and its noun_ (homework)

_2_ **23)** My sweet, distracted mother felt completely, ridiculous when she asked for a pound of

                1   2

Swiss cheese, which was impossible to get since she was at the auto parts store!

           3

#1 _two adjectives tests_

#2 _splits linking verb_ (felt) _and predicate adjective_ (ridiculous)

#3 _nonessential modifier_

Application & Enrichment
This, That, These, Those

As we learned in Level 3, *this, that, these,* and *those* are **demonstrative pronouns.**

Think of pointing at something in the store display case: "What do you want?" "I want *that.*" Demonstrative pronouns point something out or set it apart. These pronouns usually do not have antecedents.

Singular	Plural
this	these
that	those

These words can also be used as adjectives. **This** and **that** are singular modifiers; **these** and **those** are plural. They need to agree in number with the noun or pronoun they are modifying.

Examples: Incorrect: Those kind are my favorites.

Correct: That kind is my favorite. **or** Those kinds are my favorites.

Everything agrees in number: modifier, subject, verb, predicate nominative.

Incorrect: These sort of shoes hurt my feet.

Correct: This sort of shoe hurts my feet. **or** These sorts of shoes hurt my feet.

Again, notice that everything agrees in number.

The other difference between these words is that they indicate how close to or far away from the speaker the word being modified is. Imagine that you step up to the bakery counter and there are two cookies left. The one farther from you is your very favorite kind. The closer one is not only a kind you intensely dislike, but it looks like it may have sat there all day under the warmer.

"Which cookie would you like?"

"That one." *That one* means the one that's farther from you.

The same is true of *these* and *those*:

"Do you prefer these shoes or those shoes?"

"Oh, I like *these* best!"

Directions

Circle the correct choice.

1) He certainly ate enough of (that, (those)) (kind, (kinds)) of cookies.
    Note: those kinds *is correct because* cookies *is plural*

2) I have never seen (these, (this)) (types, (type)) of notebook before.
    Note: this type *is correct because* notebook *is singular*

3) We have never eaten (these, (this)) kind before.

4) The store does not sell (this, (these)) (type, (types)) of stoves any more.

5) (That, (Those)) (sort, (sorts)) of candies upset my stomach.

Directions

Choose one word from each set of parentheses to complete the sentences, making sure that all of your choices agree in number. Then write in the blank whether your completed sentence is singular or plural. Be sure to read the sentence to see if there are any clues to which number is correct!

6) Our gym class does (that, (those)) (kind, (kinds)) of exercises.
    plural

7) ((This,) These) ((brand,) brands) of tape (have, (has)) inferior quality.*
    singular

8) Nurses wear ((this,) these) type of ((shoe,) shoes).
    singular

9) Campers use (this, (these)) (sort, (sorts)) of tents.
    plural

10) Lola can do ((that,) those) ((sort,) sorts) of back dive.
    singular

Either answer could be correct for this sentence as long as all of the choices agree in number. That's because the plural of tape *is* tape. *Make sure that all word choices agree with the number (singular or plural) that your student has written in the blank.*

Comma Rules 1–5: Assessment

Directions

Insert commas where they are needed, according to the comma rules indicated for each section.
Use the lesson notes if you need help. Write **correct** if there are no changes needed.

Each correctly placed comma is worth one point. If no commas are needed, the sentence is worth one point.

Items in a Series

___
3 **1)** She was formerly on the staff of the embassies in Moscow, Berlin, Vienna,
and Madrid.

___
2 **2)** There were toys for the children, books for Mom and Dad, and a stereo for me!

___
2 **3)** During the summer, workers installed a new gym floor, an improved heating system,
and smartboards in the high school.

___
1 **4)** The weather forecaster predicted rain or sleet or snow for tomorrow.
        correct

___
3 **5)** We walked, we played, we ate, and we had a great time.

══
11

Two Adjectives Tests

___
1 **6)** She is an alert, lively puppy.

___
1 **7)** We patiently sat through a long, boring speech.

___
1 **8)** It was a raw, dark November day.

___
1 **9)** She is a bright, talented young woman.

___
1 **10)** He wore a new blue blazer to the concert.
        correct

══
5

Compound Sentence

_____**11)** I grabbed the wet dog, and Susie slammed the door before he could get away.
1

_____**12)** I gave some good advice to Jim and got some from him in return.
1   *correct*

_____**13)** The first two acts were slow-moving, but the third act is full of action.
1

_____**14)** You go ahead and I'll follow you.
1   *correct*

_____**15)** The train pulled out of the station and left me stranded there with no luggage.
1   *correct*

_____
5

Nonessential Modifiers

_____**16)** Daniel Lopez, who was offered scholarships to two colleges, will go to Yale
2   in September.

_____**17)** Daniel is the only senior who was offered two scholarships.
1   *correct*

_____**18)** My youngest brother, who was playing in the street, was almost struck by a car.
2

_____**19)** Animals frightened by thunder often try to hide.
1   *correct*

_____**20)** Friends who do favors for you may expect you to do favors for them.
1   *correct*

_____
7

Two Adjectives Tests

Directions

Underline and identify the introductory element in each sentence, using the following abbreviations:

int = interjection

part = participial phrase

prep = prepositional phrase(s)

ac = adverb clause

Insert commas where they are needed. Each correctly underlined introductory element is worth one point. Correct labeling of the introductory element is worth one point. Each correctly placed comma is worth one point.

_____ **21)** Well, be sure to ask if you need help.
3   *int*

_____ **22)** In the second part of the first period, Davis slam-dunked the ball to put us ahead.
3   *prep*

_____ **23)** Speaking in the assembly, Katy urged students to keep the school clean.
3   *part*

_____ **24)** In the newspaper, writers occasionally make grammatical mistakes.
3   *prep*

_____ **25)** While Bill was driving, our truck lurched alarmingly.
3   *ac*

_____ **26)** Having studied the comma rules in detail, Rosie aced the test.
3   *part*

_____ **27)** Why, anyone can see the man is ill!
3   *int*

_____ **28)** Since we were leaving in the morning, we went to bed early.
3   *ac*

_____ **29)** By the end of the class, the students were extremely restless.
3   *prep*

_____ **30)** Finished at the last minute, the report was poorly done.
3   *part*

_____
30

All Comma Rules

Directions

Insert commas where they are needed, according to Comma Rules 1–5. You will need to apply more than one comma rule to one of the sentences, and one sentence does not need a comma. Write ***correct*** below that one.

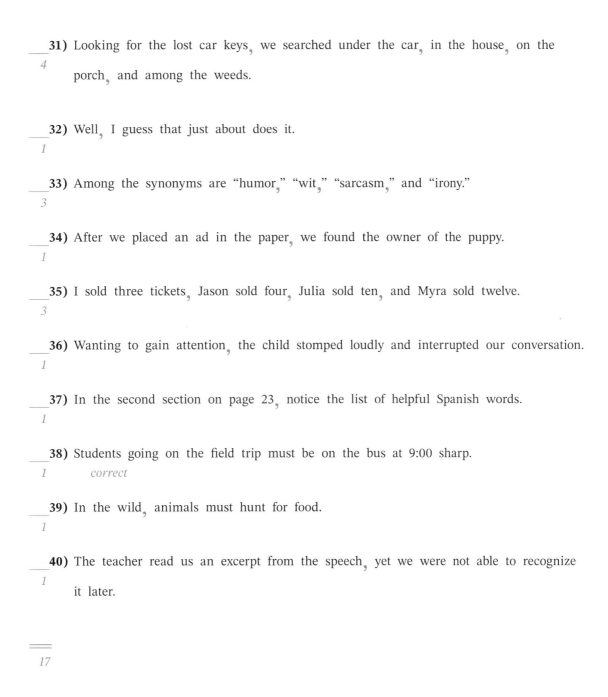

____ **31)** Looking for the lost car keys, we searched under the car, in the house, on the
4
porch, and among the weeds.

____ **32)** Well, I guess that just about does it.
1

____ **33)** Among the synonyms are "humor," "wit," "sarcasm," and "irony."
3

____ **34)** After we placed an ad in the paper, we found the owner of the puppy.
1

____ **35)** I sold three tickets, Jason sold four, Julia sold ten, and Myra sold twelve.
3

____ **36)** Wanting to gain attention, the child stomped loudly and interrupted our conversation.
1

____ **37)** In the second section on page 23, notice the list of helpful Spanish words.
1

____ **38)** Students going on the field trip must be on the bus at 9:00 sharp.
1   *correct*

____ **39)** In the wild, animals must hunt for food.
1

____ **40)** The teacher read us an excerpt from the speech, yet we were not able to recognize
1
it later.

═══
17

Directions

In each sentence below, there is a comma split. All of the commas in each sentence and the spaces below them are numbered. Identify the comma split and write its number in the space next to the sentence number. In the space under each, write what it is splitting on the appropriate line. For the correctly placed commas, write the comma rule "buzzword" in the numbered space.

Correctly identifying the comma split is worth two points. Correctly completing the lines below the sentence is worth one point each.

___2___ **41)** The exhausted, exasperated, teacher walked quickly to the faculty lounge, which was
2   1   2   3

the only place where she could find peace for a moment.

#1 ___*two adjectives tests*___
1

#2 ___*splits modifier* (exasperated) *and its noun* (teacher)___
1

#3 ___*nonessential modifier*___
1

___2___ **42)** In a kingdom by the sea, the boy in the poem, loved the main character, who was
2   1   2   3

called Annabel Lee.

#1 ___*introductory element*___
1

#2 ___*splits subject* (boy) *and verb* (loved)___
1

#3 ___*nonessential modifier*___
1

___2___ **43)** Determined to stop students from running in the halls, Mr. Calderra suspended,
2   1   2

John Griffith, Tim McGrath, and Tina Matthews.
                 3   4

#1 ___*introductory element*___
1

#2 ___*splits verb* (suspended) *and direct object* (John Griffith, etc.)___
1

#3 ___*items in a series*___
1

#4 ___*items in a series*___
1

___3___ **44)** The Great Bandini, who is undoubtedly the greatest magician on earth, showed his
_2_   1   2

fascinated audience, the most amazing trick of all time.
                     3

___ **#1**   *nonessential modifier*
_1_

___ **#2**   *nonessential modifier*
_1_

___ **#3**   *splits indirect object* (audience) *and direct object* (trick)
_1_

___1___ **45)** The student who wrote the best essay was, the winner of the Literary Award, and he
_2_   1   2

received a scholarship, a cash prize, and a certificate.
                     3   4

___ **#1**   *splits linking verb* (was) *and predicate nominative* (winner)
_1_

___ **#2**   *compound sentence*
_1_

___ **#3**   *items in a series*
_1_

___ **#4**   *items in a series*
_1_

.

===
_27_

=== *Total Points* $\dfrac{82}{102} = 80\%$
_102_

Comma Rules 6, 7, and 8

Lesson 5: Comma Rules 6, 7, and 8

These comma rules all have to do with things that interrupt the flow of a sentence. Because they interrupt the flow, they are set apart with commas. If they are in the middle of the sentence, they will need two commas—one before and one after. If they are at the beginning or the end of the sentence, they will only need one.

Comma Rule 6: Appositives

As we learned in Level 4, an appositive is a noun or pronoun that restates another noun or pronoun in a sentence. An appositive phrase includes the noun or pronoun plus anything modifying it. It is usually located after the noun or pronoun it is restating and helps to describe it by giving further information about it.*

Examples: I often play tennis, a lively game.
The appositive phrase a lively game *is another name for* tennis *and further describes it.*

My cousin, Zoe Skelton, lives in England.
The appositive Zoe Skelton *further describes* cousin.

The Pride of the Yankees is a movie about Lou Gehrig, a famous baseball player.
The appositive phrase a famous baseball player *tells us more about* Lou Gehrig.

*Refer to your notes from Level 4 on appositives and appositive phrases if needed.

Sometimes an appositive is so closely related to the noun it is restating that it does not need to be set off by commas. If you're not sure whether you need a comma or not, try reading the sentence very dramatically, like a television newscaster. You will naturally pause if you need a comma. If you don't need to pause, you don't need a comma.

Each of these sentences includes an appositive or appositive phrase, but they are so connected to the original noun or pronoun that no comma is necessary.

Examples: My sister Elizabeth is left-handed. (*Elizabeth* = appositive of *My sister*)

We girls are going shopping. (*girls* = appositive of *We*)

The writer Mark Twain is dead. (*Mark Twain* = appositive of *writer*)

Note: If the appositive phrase is a **title** that is already set off by either italics or quotation marks (more on this in Lesson 9), then commas should not be used around that title.

Examples: My favorite movie *Tin Men* isn't very well known.

My friend insisted we listen to his new song "Relax and Smile" before our performance.

Comma Rule 7: Direct Address

Direct address means any name you call someone when you are speaking directly to them. It can be their proper name, a nickname, or another form of address.

Examples: The program, Juan, has been changed. (direct address = *Juan*)

Miss Bates, may I leave early? (direct address = *Miss Bates*)

Please get down from the counter, Pumpkin. (direct address = *Pumpkin*)

My fellow students, I am proud to be your valedictorian.
(direct address = *My fellow students)*

Comma Rule 8: Parenthetical Expression

We use many expressions to add emotion and nuance to our language. These usually don't serve any other specific grammatical purpose in a sentence, and the sentence would make just as much sense without them. They are called **parenthetical expressions** because they are the kind of information that you might see in parentheses. These include commonly used expressions like "after all," "on the other hand," or "I think." Because they are nonessential, they should be set off from the rest of the sentence with commas.

Examples: He didn't, however, keep his promise. (parenthetical expression = *however*)

After all, you won the contest! (parenthetical expression = *After all*)

American men, in general, seem to prefer dark suits.
(parenthetical expression = *in general*)

Comma Rules 6, 7, and 8: Exercise A

Directions

Underline the appositive or appositive phrase. Draw an arrow to the noun or pronoun it restates.
Insert commas where necessary.

1) Jack, <u>my little cousin</u>, still prefers nursery rhymes.

2) My friend <u>Mary Jo</u> will visit us soon.

3) Beverly Cleary, <u>author of the Ramona Quimby stories</u>, is a popular children's writer.

4) Have you met Nina Jackson, <u>my best friend</u>?

5) Science, <u>my favorite subject</u>, gets more fun each year!

6) The Ladipo twins, <u>members of the rugby team</u>, have to report for practice soon.

7) Archimedes, <u>the Greek physicist</u>, made a great discovery by placing a gold crown in a tub of water.

8) The boys had fun working on the car, <u>a dilapidated old wreck</u>.

9) Both of the animals, <u>a horse and a cow</u>, were rescued from the fire.

10) A black funnel-shaped cloud, <u>the sign of a tornado</u>, sent everyone running for shelter.

Directions

Rewrite each pair of sentences into a single sentence containing an appositive or an appositive phrase. Be sure to add commas where necessary.

Example: Jill Douglas is the mayor of our town. She will speak next.

Jill Douglas, mayor of our town, will speak next.

Answers will vary. Be sure each sentence contains an appositive or appositive phrase and doesn't change the meaning of the original sentences. One possible solution is given.

11) The fastest runner is Penny Nguyen. She is on the track team.

The fastest runner, Penny Nguyen, is on the track team.

12) We have a favorite horse. Her name is Daisy and she won the race.

Our favorite horse, Daisy, won the race.

13) The author is Mark Twain. He knew a lot about people.

The author Mark Twain knew a lot about people.

14) The girl in the third row is Paula. She likes to hike.

Paula, the girl in the third row, likes to hike.

15) There was only one hit against Lester. It was a single.

There was only one hit, a single, against Lester.

Directions

Insert commas where they are needed.

16) Mom, have you met Mrs. Gillespie?

17) On the other hand, I'd rather have the day off.

18) Dinner, Madame, is served.

Directions

In each sentence below, there is a comma split. All of the commas in each sentence and the lines below them are numbered. Identify the comma split and write its number in the space next to the sentence number. On the lines under each, write what the comma is splitting on the appropriate line. For the correctly placed commas, write the comma rule "buzzword" on the numbered line.

_1_ **19)** Since the boy who was the winner of the skating competition, had only been training for a
                                                                1

short while, some of the other competitors were jealous, or at least they envied his
              2   3

apparently effortless, natural style.
                      4

#1 _splits subject_ (boy) _and verb_ (had been training)

#2 _introductory elements_

#3 _compound sentence_

#4 _two adjectives tests_

_5_ **20)** In a short, clear memo to her workers, Ms. Stone described all the things she thought were wrong
                  1   2

with the company, how they had gotten that way, and exactly what, could be done about them.
                  3   4   5

#1 _two adjectives tests_

#2 _introductory elements_

#3 _items in a series_

#4 _items in a series_

#5 _splits subject_ (what) _and verb_ (could be done)

_4_ **21)** Jack, my little cousin, still enjoys nursery rhymes, yet he is growing every day, more and
          1   2   3   4

more mature.

#1 _appositive_

#2 _appositive_

#3 _compound sentence_

#4 _splits linking verb_ (is growing) _and predicate adjective_ (mature)

Comma Rules 6, 7, and 8: Exercise B

Directions

Underline the appositives and appositive phrases in the passage below. Insert commas where they are needed.

Yesterday at dawn, my family was startled out of bed by a loud screech of tires, my uncle Jasper's car pulling into our driveway. Soon we heard voices in the hallway, our relatives all talking at once. Sadie, my aunt, asked, "Oh, is this pretty house where your brother Bob lives? Won't they be surprised to see us, their favorite relatives?"

Sparky, our little cocker spaniel, expressed our surprise by barking noisily at the intruders, our uninvited and unexpected relatives. Then Bonecrusher, their Saint Bernard, jumped forward and tried to make breakfast out of Sparky! Dad untangled the snarling animals and tied both of them, Sparky and Bonecrusher, in the backyard. Mortal enemies on sight, the dogs spent the rest of the day growling and yapping at each other.

A minor incident, that fight was only the beginning of the turmoil in our house. Wilbur, Uncle Jasper's youngest boy, took an immediate liking to a hand-painted vase, a treasured heirloom, and dashed it to smithereens. While Aunt Sadie was apologizing for Wilbur, Uncle Jasper was chasing Sylvester, his oldest boy. Sylvester, meanwhile, was chasing my sister Beth so he could cut her hair with the kitchen scissors!

Just before leaving the house, a place I used to call "Home Sweet Home," Uncle Jasper said, "We're going to spend our whole vacation, two weeks, with you!" To be polite, we have to stay home and play nifty games, particularly Monopoly and Chinese checkers. Even our family's bedtime, formerly 10:00, has changed to midnight. And since Aunt Sadie has insomnia, a condition which prevents her from sleeping past 5:00 in the morning, everybody gets up for an early breakfast. My heart sinks when I think about their visit, a full two weeks.

But yesterday, Mom, a wonderfully wise person, smiled at my complaints. "Take heart, Danny, my son," she said. "We will have our revenge! Our day will come at about 2:00 in the afternoon on a Thursday in November, Thanksgiving, when—totally unannounced—we'll just drop in on THEM!"

Directions

Use each of the following items as an appositive or appositive phrase in sentences of your own. Write ten separate sentences, one for each item below. Be sure to insert commas where they are needed.

Answers will vary.

Example: Hawaiian pizza

Everybody's favorite, Hawaiian pizza, is the best pizza ever!
(Your sentences don't have to be true!)

1) Linda

2) a nuisance

3) my neighbor

4) a good teacher

5) Austin and Victor

6) the life of the party

7) a girl sitting near me

8) the candidate to select

9) a book for children

10) the man you should meet

Directions

In each sentence below, there is a comma split. All of the commas in each sentence and the lines below them are numbered. Identify the comma split and write its number in the space next to the sentence number. On the numbered lines under each, write what the comma is splitting. For the correctly placed commas, write the comma rule "buzzword" on the numbered line.

_3_ **11)** My neighbor's relatives, an interesting group, visit them each summer with an assortment
1   2

of equally peculiar, friends.
3

#1 _appositive_

#2 _appositive_

#3 _splits modifier_ (peculiar) _and its noun_ (friends)

_3_ **12)** During the early part of last June, they were looking forward to a few weeks of complete,
1   2

total relaxation when they answered, an unexpected knock at the door.
3

#1 _introductory element_

#2 _two adjectives tests_

#3 _splits verb_ (answered) _and direct object_ (knock)

_4_ **13)** Standing there in all their splendor of baggy Bermuda shorts, knobby knees, and friendly
1   2

grins were Uncle Herbert and his large, boisterous, family.
3   4

#1 _items in a series_

#2 _items in a series_

#3 _two adjectives tests_

#4 _splits modifier_ (boisterous) _and its noun_ (family)

Comma Rules 6, 7, and 8: Exercise C

Directions

Underline the interrupters in the following sentences. Identify them in the space provided below each sentence using the following abbreviations:

app = appositive or appositive phrase

da = direct address

pe = parenthetical expression

Insert commas where they are needed.

1) The story, in my opinion, is much too long and complicated.

pe

2) You scoundrel, what do you mean by trying to cheat your friends?

da

3) When Mr. Kean, my geography teacher, visited Indiana, he toured the beautiful campus of Indiana University.

app

4) Richie, leave the room and shut the door.

da

5) Mathematics, I'm afraid, is not my best subject.

pe

6) Little Women, a classic book for young people, was a part of my growing up.

app

7) You will stay, I hope, as long as you can.

pe

8) Do you remember, Patty, what Romeo's last name is?

da

9) Modern highways, for example, are marvelous feats of engineering.

pe

10) May I go to the movies, Dad?

da

Directions

In each sentence below, there is a comma split. All of the commas in each sentence and the lines below them are numbered. Identify the comma split and write its number in the space next to the sentence number. On the numbered lines under each, write what the comma is splitting on. For the correctly placed commas, write the comma rule "buzzword" on the numbered line.

___4___ **11)** What, in your opinion, was the cause of the economic crash of 1929, and why didn't the
            1   2   3

people in charge of the stock market, do anything about it?
                                 4

#1 _parenthetical expression_

#2 _parenthetical expression_

#3 _compound sentence_

#4 _splits subject_ (people) _and verb_ (do)

___6___ **12)** My hair dryer, which I bought three years ago, has put out more hot air than any
                     1   2

political candidate, but this morning, if you can believe it, it decided, to stop working!
                3   4   5   6

#1 _nonessestial modifier_

#2 _nonessestial modifier_

#3 _compound sentence_

#4 _parenthetical expression_

#5 _parenthetical expression_

#6 _splits verb_ (decided) _and direct object_ (to stop working)

___1___ **13)** Anybody who has ever tried to eat spaghetti at a fancy restaurant, knows that, no matter
                                                    1   2

what, you'll end up with sauce all over your chin, down your shirt, and on the tablecloth.
             3   4   5

#1 _splits subject_ (anybody) _and verb_ (knows)

#2 _parenthetical expression_

#3 _parenthetical expression_

#4 _items in a series_

#5 _items in a series_

Application & Enrichment
Transitional Devices

As we've learned, parenthetical expressions are not essential to understanding a sentence. Technically, the sentence will make perfect grammatical sense without them. However, in a dialog or a paragraph including more than one sentence, they can provide essential context to understand what's going on.

Look at the sample conversation below about Mrs. Dragonbottom, the extremely mean grammar teacher. Is it difficult to follow? It appears to say one thing and then immediately says just the opposite!

1) Mrs. Dragonbottom is the meanest teacher in this whole school!

2) She's an absolute sweetheart!

3) She can be rather vindictive when she is crossed.

4) She gave me a detention just for setting fire to Martha Sue's pigtails!

5) She's a mean old lady!

6) I don't think I've ever known anybody as mean as Mrs. Dragonbottom.

7) She rescued that poor little lost puppy last week.

8) That doesn't excuse all the other stuff she does.

9) When Billy knocked over the outhouse, she called his mom!

10) Billy was grounded until his 21st birthday!

Now read through each sentence in the conversation again, but add the parenthetical expressions, in order, to the beginning of each sentence. Is it still hard to follow?

1) As I was saying

2) On the contrary

3) Of course

4) For instance

5) If you ask me

6) To tell the truth

7) On the other hand

8) However

9) For example

10) In fact

The parenthetical expressions make what is being said much clearer! When used in this way, parenthetical expressions are known as **transitional devices**. Using transitional devices is essential for clear writing when you are contrasting information or providing different opinions. They help your reader to see that you are changing directions, and they are able to follow along.

For more practice, have a conversation with your instructor about any topic you enjoy: books, movies, sports, or anything at all. Take turns making up sentences about the topic. Make your conversation as silly or as serious as you'd like. The only rule is that you have to include the next transitional device from the list above in your sentence!

Transitional devices provide indispensable support to those who are reading or listening to your writing or speech. Try to use them as often as necessary to make your communication as clear as it can be.

Comma Rules 6, 7, and 8: Assessment

Comma Rule 6: Appositives and Appositive Phrases

Directions

Insert commas where they are needed. Write **correct** underneath the sentence if there are no errors.

Each correctly placed comma is worth one point. If no commas are needed, the sentence is worth one point

___ **1)** Shana Alexander, one-time editor of McCall's, was the main speaker.
2

___ **2)** We have a figurine made of clay from Kilimanjaro, Africa's highest mountain.
1

___ **3)** The whole class listened to my best friend Jane give her speech.
1   *Correct*

___ **4)** Saint Augustine, the oldest city in the United States, has many narrow streets.
2

___ **5)** Sugar cane, an important Florida crop, may be shipped refined or raw.
2

___ **6)** Do you own a thesaurus, a dictionary of synonyms and antonyms?
1

___ **7)** At North Cape, the northernmost point of Europe, the sun does not set from the
2   middle of May until the end of July.

___ **8)** The American mastodon, an extinct elephant-like animal, was hunted by
2   primitive man.

___ **9)** John F. Kennedy's brother Robert was assassinated during a presidential campaign.
1   *Correct*

___ **10)** At Thermopylae, a narrow pass in eastern Greece, a band of three hundred
2   Spartans faced an army of thousands from Persia.

___
16

Comma Rule 7: Direct Address

Directions

Insert commas where they are needed.

Each correctly placed comma is worth one point.

____ **11)** Gillian, why do you call your cat Teddy Roosevelt?
  1

____ **12)** Stop this incessant chatter, class.
  1

____ **13)** We, my fellow graduates, will be the leaders of the next generation.
  2

____ **14)** Professor Adams, when was the Battle of Marathon?
  1

____ **15)** What is your opinion of the candidates, Laura?
  1

____ **16)** Dad, may I borrow the car?
  1

____ **17)** Where, my dear Mr. Nelson, do you think you are?
  2

____ **18)** Senator Smith, I have a proposal for improving our state.
  1

____ **19)** Lisa, you really need to apologize.
  1

____ **20)** You know that cats aren't allowed on the counter, Pixie!
  1

══
12

Comma Rule 8: Parenthetical Expressions

Directions

Insert commas where they are needed.

Each correctly placed comma is worth one point.

___ **21)** Yes, there are many constellations visible in the summer.
  1

___ **22)** For instance, on a summer night, you can see the Scorpion and the Serpent.
  1

___ **23)** To be sure, we should not fail to mention the Milky Way.
  1

___ **24)** The Milky Way, in fact, is more impressive in the summer than at any other time.
  2

___ **25)** Of course, Hercules is an interesting constellation.
  1

___ **26)** Studying the constellations is, in my opinion, a most interesting pastime.
  2

___ **27)** It does take some imagination, however, to pick out some of them.
  2

___ **28)** The Archer, for example, is hard to perceive.
  2

___ **29)** The Scorpion, on the other hand, is quite clearly outlined.
  2

___ **30)** Astronomy, I think, is a fascinating career.
  2

___
16

All Comma Rules 1–8

Directions

Insert commas where they are needed. Write **correct** underneath the sentence if there are no errors.

Each correctly placed comma is worth one point. If no commas are needed, the sentence is worth one point.

____ **31)** The whole family, several friends, and some relatives from out of state came for
2   dinner on Sunday.

____ **32)** Mom made a delicious gourmet meal, and we sat down at a table loaded with food.
1

____ **33)** Yes, we all ate way too much!
1

____ **34)** I especially loved the golden-brown, piping-hot, home-baked rolls.
2

____ **35)** My dad, who is trying to lose a few pounds, started off with a generous serving
2   of salad.

____ **36)** Since he'd only eaten salad, he decided to have a "tiny taste" of everything else.
1

____ **37)** The "tiny taste," a generous serving of everything edible on the table, filled his plate!
2

____ **38)** His diet, needless to say, was blown sky high for the day.
2

____ **39)** Cutting himself a large piece of lemon meringue pie, Dad declared that his diet
1   would start first thing the next morning.

____ **40)** Dinners that Mom makes on festive occasions are always fatal to Dad's diet!
1   *Correct*

‗‗
15

Directions

In each sentence below, there is a comma split. All of the commas in each sentence and the spaces below them are numbered. Identify the comma split and write its number in the space next to the sentence number. In the space under each, write what it is splitting on the appropriate line. For the correctly placed commas, write the comma rule "buzzword" in the numbered space.

Correctly identifying the comma split is worth two points. Correctly completing the lines below the sentence is worth one point each.

___4___ **41)** Yes, we all sat around looking at old yearbooks, laughing at the funny hair styles we
_2_   1   2

        wore, and secretly wishing with all our hearts, that we could go back to those good old
               3   4

        days for a while.

    ___ **#1**   *introductory elements* _____
    1

    ___ **#2**   *items in a series* _____
    1

    ___ **#3**   *items in a series* _____
    1

    ___ **#4**   *splits verb* (wishing) *and direct object* (that we could go...)
    1

___1___ **42)** The character in the play who had all the money and fame, was the one whom we most
_2_   1

        suspected, but the real murderer was a quiet, mousy person whom no one even noticed!
              2   3

    ___ **#1**   *splits subject* (character) *and verb* (was) _____
    1

    ___ **#2**   *compound sentence* _____
    1

    ___ **#3**   *two adjectives tests* _____
    1

___4___ **43)** John, the most able debater on the team, appeared to be stumped for an answer until
_2_   1   2

        one of the youngest, least-experienced, members of the team saved the day.
                     3   4

    ___ **#1**   *appositive* _____
    1

    ___ **#2**   *appositive* _____
    1

    ___ **#3**   *two adjectives tests* _____
    1

    ___ **#4**   *splits modifier* (least-experienced) *and its noun* (members)
    1

_4_ **44)** Before Albert was old enough to get a license, he had already picked out his car, a used

2   1   2

Chevrolet with 40,000 miles on it, and started, a savings account for the down payment

3   4

with his own money.

___ **#1** _introductory element_ _____
1

___ **#2** _appositive_ _____
1

___ **#3** _appositive_ _____
1

___ **#4** _splits verb_ (stated) _and direct object_ (account) _____
1

___
_23_

For **five points extra credit**, diagram the following sentence:

Any student of this course in grammar should know the structure of the sentence and the
function of every word in it.

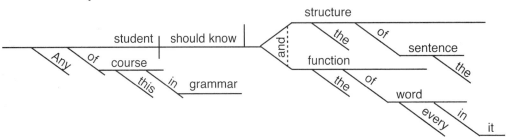

___ _Total Points_ $\dfrac{66}{82} = 80\%$
_82_

Comma Rules 9, 10, and 11

Lesson 6: Comma Rules 9, 10, and 11

The comma rules in this final set are easy, straightforward situations with few exceptions.

Comma Rule 9: Dates & Addresses

Use commas to separate items in dates and addresses, and also put a comma after the last item in the date or address if the sentence continues.

Examples: My family moved to Knoxville, Tennessee, on Monday, May 4, 1964.
On May 4, 1964, I bought a car at Cisco Cadillac, 645 Commerce Street, Knoxville, Tennessee 20200.

You should not put a comma between the state and zip code in an address, but all other parts should be separated by commas.

If the items in your address or date are separated by prepositions, they should not also be separated by commas.

Example: I moved to 330 Elm Street in Waynesville, Illinois. (no comma after *Elm Street*)

Comma Rule 10: Salutations and Closings

Use a comma after the salutation of an informal letter or email (use a colon for business letters). Use a comma after the closing of any letter or email.

Examples: Dear Jim, (friendly letter)
Dear Doctor Morgan: (business letter)
Truly yours,
Love and kisses,
Sincerely,

What determines whether or not a letter or email is business or friendly is not how well you know the person you are writing to. It is determined by the intent of the communication. If the content is social, it is a friendly letter or email, even if you are writing to someone you have never met. If the content is business-related, it's a business letter or email, even if you are writing to your old college roommate who now does your taxes.

Comma Rule 11: Post-Nominal Letters

Post-nominal letters are letters used after a name to indicate specific statuses, academic degrees, honorary titles, and other information. Use a comma between the name and first set of letters. If there is more than one set of post-nominal letters, put a comma after each set. Use a comma after the final set of letters if the sentence continues.

Suffixes are not the same as post-nominal letters. Suffixes are part of a person's or business's proper name, such as Jr., Sr, III, Inc., LLC, or Ltd. Do not use a comma with suffixes.

Examples: Alicia Zweiback, Esq.
Martin Luther King Jr.
Bob Geldof, KBE
Math-U-See Inc.
Robert Herrera Jr., MD
Herr's Plumbing LLC
Sir Winston Leonard Spencer Churchill, KG, OM, CH, TD, DL, FRS, RA
Elizabeth II

Comma Rules 9, 10, and 11: Exercise A

Directions

Insert commas where they are needed.

1) 443 North University Avenue, Lansing, Michigan 48103

2) 1900 Logan Road, Linden, New Jersey 07036

3) Monday, August 5, 1991

4) after January 1, 1984

5) 379 Scott Avenue, Salt Lake City, Utah 85115

6) Michigan Avenue at Twelfth Street, Chicago, Illinois

7) Thanksgiving Day, 1978

8) from June 23, 1989, to January 2, 1990

9) either Tuesday, September 3, or Saturday, September 7

10) Box 147, Rapid City, South Dakota

11) The building on the corner of Market Street and Highland Avenue in Akron, Ohio, is where my grandfather was born.

12) Sincerely yours,

13) Dear Jean, (in a letter thanking her for a baby shower gift)

14) Dear George: (in a letter asking your financial adviser for information on the stock market)

15) The Founding Fathers of the United States signed the Declaration of Independence in Philadelphia, Pennsylvania, on July 4, 1776.

16) The party will be on Friday, July 9, in Wheeling, West Virginia, at 7:00 in the evening.

Directions

In each sentence below, there is a comma split. All of the commas in each sentence and the lines below them are numbered. Identify the comma split and write its number in the space next to the sentence number. On the lines under each, write what the comma is splitting on the appropriate line. For the correctly placed commas, write the comma rule "buzzword" on the numbered line.

_3_ **17)** In July, 1776, Thomas Jefferson and the other Founding Fathers, gave us the
      1   2   3

Declaration of Independence.

#1 _dates & addresses_

#2 _dates & addresses_

#3 _splits subject_ (Thomas Jefferson and the Founding Fathers)

and verb (gave)

_1_ **18)** The men at the Continental Congress in Philadelphia, voted on a document which remains
                                                1

one of the most famous, revered writings of all time, but they probably didn't realize that
                  2   3

at the time.

#1 _splits subject_ (men) _and verb_ (voted)

#2 _two adjectives tests_

#3 _compound sentence_

_3_ **19)** When the Declaration was finally signed on July 4, 1776, they surely thought, that the world
                                              1   2   3

would soon forget what they had done on that hot, humid day.
                                                4

#1 _dates & addresses_

#2 _dates & addresses_

#3 _splits verb_ (thought) _and direct object_ (that the world...)

#4 _two adjectives tests_

Comma Rules 9, 10, and 11: Exercise B

Directions
Insert commas where they are needed.

1) The first Boston Marathon was held on April 19, 1897.

2) Are you talking about Kansas City, Kansas, or Kansas City, Missouri?

3) Sherlock Holmes supposedly lived at 221B Baker Street, London, England.

4) Please reply to Campbell and Jones Inc., 135 South LaSalle Street, Chicago, Illinois 60603.

5) He was born on April 3, 1963, which makes him an Aries.

6) Ed's address is 4652 Orchard Street, Oakland, California.

7) We're going to the museum on Thursday, May 5.

8) Does this address say Gary, Indiana, or Cary, Illinois?

9) My older brother hasn't had many birthdays because he was born on February 29, 1980.

10) Someday, my address will be 1600 Pennsylvania Avenue, Washington, D.C.

Directions

Using all of the comma rules you have learned, insert commas where they are needed. Below the sentence, write the buzzword for each rule you use. Be alert! One sentence applies two different comma rules.

11) Since Susan's visit was to be a short one, we wanted to do something special each day.

introductory element

12) A luncheon was held in her honor, and all of her high school buddies were there.

compound sentence

13) Claiming to be totally surprised, Susan had a terrific time.

introductory element

14) At her table were Maria, Stacey, Beth, and Renee.

items in a series

15) Since no one had plans for the evening, we talked until it was quite late.

introductory element

16) The waiter cleared our table, but we sat over coffee and talked for hours.

compound sentence

17) Susan, who was a very appreciative guest, said she had never had so much fun.

nonessential modifier

18) On Saturday, June 10, we got together with some of our old neighbors.

dates & addresses

19) Yes, even old Mrs. Bates was there!

introductory element

20) After many hours of gossip, memories, and laughter, we took Susan to the airport.

items in a series, introductory element

Directions

In each sentence below, there is a comma split. All of the commas in each sentence and the lines below them are numbered. Identify the comma split and write its number in the space next to the sentence number. On the numbered lines under each, write what the comma is splitting. For the correctly placed commas, write the comma rule "buzzword" on the numbered line.

_4_ **21)** John, my next-door neighbor, is having a party this weekend, but he is extremely, nervous
    1   2   3   4

about the arrangements.

   #1 _appositive phrase_

   #2 _appositive phrase_

   #3 _compound sentence_

   #4 _splits linking verb_ (is) _and predicate adjective_ (nervous)

_1_ **22)** He has invited, all his closest, most intimate friends to a gathering on Friday, February 6th.
                1   2   3

   #1 _splits verb_ (invited) _and direct object_ (friends)

   #2 _two adjectives tests_

   #3 _dates & addresses_

_3_ **23)** The refreshments, the music, and all the games, have been gathered together, and we all
                    1   2   3   4

expect to have a wild, crazy time!
                     5

   #1 _items in a series_

   #2 _items in a series_

   #3 _splits subject_ (games) _and verb_ (have been gathered)

   #4 _compound sentence_

   #5 _two adjectives tests_

Comma Rules 9, 10, and 11: Exercise C

Directions

Insert commas where they are needed.

1) My cousins were both born on September 6, 2003.

2) Why is 10 Downing Street, London, famous?

3) Eleanor Roosevelt was born on October 11, 1884, and died on November 7, 1962.

4) Where were you on Saturday, June 23, 2018?

5) Reno, Nevada, is farther west than Los Angeles, California.

6) Saturday, July 26, is Kathryn's birthday party.

7) The best hot dogs on earth are at Petey's, 110 Washington Street, Elm Forest, Illinois.

8) Address your letter to the Chicago Sun-Times, 401 North Wabash Avenue, Chicago, Illinois 60611.

9) We lived at 130 Rand Road, Austin, Texas, from May 1, 1993, to April 30, 1997.

10) The only historical date I can remember is July 4, 1776.

Directions

Using all of the comma rules you have learned, insert commas where they are needed. Below the sentence, write the buzzword for each rule you use.

11) Sophie lives on a farm, and she invited us to visit her last weekend.

compound sentence

12) Although we had seen many farms, staying at one was a new experience.

introductory element

13) It was great fun, in my opinion, to see all the cows, horses, pigs, and chickens.

parenthetical expression, items in a series

14) When the roosters began to crow at dawn, the farm seemed to come to life.

introductory element

15) Breakfast was very early so that we could get to the barn to see the milking machine, feed the pigs, and scatter feed for the chickens.

items in a series

16) Dinner was at noon and we had never had such heaping platters of mashed potatoes, fried chicken, fresh peas, and homemade blueberry muffins.

items in a series

17) After we had eaten our dessert, we stretched out under a big, leafy tree and went to sleep.

introductory element, two adjectives tests

18) Since it was a warm, humid afternoon, we were glad to go for a cool, refreshing swim.

two adjectives tests, introductory element, two adjectives tests

19) Getting ready for bed that night, we agreed that the farm was the perfect vacation spot.

introductory element

20) Completely exhausted by our day outdoors, we were happy to tumble into bed early.

introductory element

Directions

In each sentence below, there is a comma split. All of the commas in each sentence and the lines below them are numbered. Identify the comma split and write its number in the space next to the sentence number. On the numbered lines under each, write what the comma is splitting on. For the correctly placed commas, write the comma rule "buzzword" on the numbered line.

_3_ **21)** Sherlock Holmes, who is one of my favorite fictional characters, solved, hundreds of
                          1   2   3

difficult mysteries with the help of Dr. Watson.

#1 _nonessential modifier_

#2 _nonessential modifier_

#3 _splits verb (solved) and direct object (hundreds)_

_1_ **22)** Holmes and Watson were, extremely clever when it came to dealing with dangerous, vicious
                              1   2

criminals, and they put their share of them behind bars.
         3

#1 _splits linking verb (were) and predicate adjective (clever)_

#2 _two adjectives tests_

#3 _compound sentence_

_3_ **23)** Since the middle of the 19th century, readers have thrilled to the workings of Holmes's
                                            1

precise, computer-like, mind as he solved crime after crime.
       2   3

#1 _introductory elements_

#2 _two adjectives tests_

#3 _splits modifier (computer-like) and its noun (mind)_

Misplaced Modifiers

We have talked quite a bit about adding modifiers to sentences to make them more vivid for the reader. It's important to make sure that our modifiers are modifying the words we want them to—otherwise we can be left with some confusing (and sometimes funny) sentences! Remember that any time your reader has to stop and wonder what you mean, you have created a stumbling block for their understanding.

Unclear descriptors like these are called **misplaced modifiers**. The confusion is easily cleared up by asking ourselves some questions about what is being described. Look at the following examples:

Example: Short and chubby, Christopher Robin loved Winnie the Pooh.
Who is short and chubby? Christopher Robin or Pooh?

The runner flopped to the ground gasping for breath.
Who or what was gasping for breath—the runner or the ground?

To clear up the confusion, rewrite the sentence so that the modifier is next to (or at least close to) the word it is modifying. In the first example above, we may think Christopher Robin is short and chubby because that is the first noun following the compound modifier. This can easily be fixed in one of the following ways:

Example: Short and chubby, Christopher Robin loved Winnie the Pooh.

Better:
Short and chubby, Winnie the Pooh was loved by Christopher Robin.

Or:
Christopher Robin loved short, chubby Winnie the Pooh.

The same is true in the second sentence—the participial phrase *gasping for breath* is closer to *ground* than it is to *runner*.

Example: The runner flopped to the ground gasping for breath.

Better:
Gasping for breath, the runner flopped to the ground.

Or:
The runner, gasping for breath, flopped to the ground.

In both of these examples, the modifying phrase has been moved to come immediately before or after the word being modified. The reader can easily understand what is being described.

Directions

Rewrite each sentence so that the modifier (adjective phrase, participial phrase, or adverbial phrase) is correctly placed near or next to the thing being described. Rearrange the sentence or change words, if necessary, to make the sentence flow.

Answers will vary. One possible solution is provided.

1) Crying loudly, Mom comforted the upset baby.

Crying loudly, the upset baby looked to Mom for comfort.

2) Greasy and cheesy, we needed napkins after eating the pizza.

After eating the greasy, cheesy pizza, we needed napkins.

3) The cat left his hair everywhere long and fuzzy.

Long and fuzzy, the cat's hair was left everywhere.

4) Swinging from tree to tree, the kids laughed at the acrobatic monkeys.

The kids laughed at the acrobatic monkeys swinging from tree to tree.

5) Reading my book, the day slipped away from me.

The day slipped away from me as I read my book.

6) The traffic gave me a headache, beeping and screeching.

The beeping and screeching traffic gave me a headache.

7) Limping dramatically, the finish line was crossed by the final participant.

Limping dramatically, the final participant crossed the finish line.

8) The lizard sat on a stone basking in the sun.

The lizard, basking in the sun, sat on a stone.

9) The burrito was served to the guest that was extra spicy.

The burrito that was extra spicy was served to the guest.

10) Darting and whirling, the evening sky was filled with swallows.

The evening sky was filled with darting and whirling swallows.

All Comma Rules: Assessment

Comma Rule 1: Items in a Series

Directions

Insert commas where they are needed. Write **correct** underneath the sentence if there are no errors. Remember to look back at the lesson notes if you need help!

Each correctly placed comma is worth one point. If no commas are needed, the sentence is worth one point

_____ **1)** Jim and Ted and Bill are my best friends among all my classmates.
1   *Correct*

_____ **2)** Today's connected homes include smart TVs, virtual assistants, and maybe even a
2   wifi-connected refrigerator.

_____ **3)** A considerate person listens when others are speaking, thinks carefully before saying
2   anything, and tries not to hurt anyone's feelings.

_____ **4)** We noticed unsightly soda cups, fast food wrappers, and torn plastic all along the road.
2

_____ **5)** I hope for a new laptop or a mountain bike or a skateboard for my birthday.
1   *Correct*

_____
8

Comma Rule 2: Two Adjectives Tests

Directions

Insert commas where they are needed. Write **correct** underneath the sentence if there are no errors.

Each correctly placed comma is worth one point. If no commas are needed, the sentence is worth one point

_____ **6)** Everyone stared at the king's priceless crown.
1   *Correct*

_____ **7)** The wagon train approached lonely, wild, mountainous terrain.
2

_____ **8)** Port Townsend is a friendly, unsophisticated little town.
1

_____ **9)** The sleek, long-haired, orange cat had a pudgy, tabby brother from the same litter.
3

_____ **10)** The old grandfather clock struck midnight.
1   *Correct*

_____
8

Comma Rule 3: Compound Sentences

Directions

Insert commas where they are needed. Write **correct** underneath the sentence if there are no errors.

Each correctly placed comma is worth one point. If no commas are needed, the sentence is worth one point

___**11)** The long drought that had worried farmers finally ended, and day after day the
1   rain came down in sheets.

___**12)** The beds of streams that had been dry came to life, and the caked soil became
1   green again.

___**13)** Small streams became raging rivers and greedily engulfed the countryside.
1   *Correct*

___**14)** The levees broke and towns were flooded.
1   *Correct*

___**15)** We thought the drought would never end, but it finally did.
1

___
5

Comma Rule 4: Nonessential Modifiers

Directions

Insert commas where they are needed. Write **correct** underneath the sentence if there are no errors.

Each correctly placed comma is worth one point. If no commas are needed, the sentence is worth one point

___**16)** Situations in which students cut school should be investigated.
1   *Correct*

___**17)** Senator Murphy, hoping for passage of her bill, talked to several legislators.
2

___**18)** All buildings which had been declared unsafe were torn down.
1   *Correct*

___**19)** I wish the new friend we made at Sandi's party would call us!
1   *Correct*

___**20)** The young salesperson, desperately trying to make a sale, talked for five minutes.
2

___
7

Comma Rule 5: Introductory Elements

Directions

Insert commas where they are needed. Write **correct** underneath the sentence if there are no errors.

Each correctly placed comma is worth one point. If no commas are needed, the sentence is worth one point

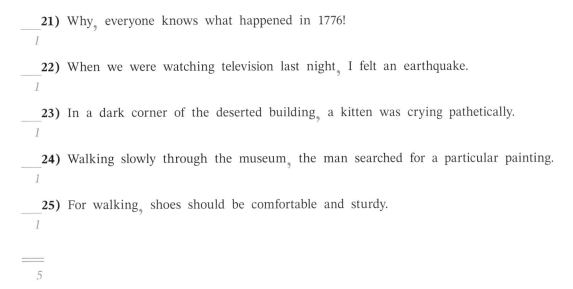

___ **21)** Why, everyone knows what happened in 1776!
1

___ **22)** When we were watching television last night, I felt an earthquake.
1

___ **23)** In a dark corner of the deserted building, a kitten was crying pathetically.
1

___ **24)** Walking slowly through the museum, the man searched for a particular painting.
1

___ **25)** For walking, shoes should be comfortable and sturdy.
1

═══
5

Comma Rules 6, 7, and 8: Appositives, Direct Address, and Parenthetical Expressions

Directions

Underline the interrupter in each sentence below. Insert commas where they are needed. Identify the interrupter below each sentence. Use the following abbreviations:

> ***app*** = appositive
>
> ***da*** = direct address
>
> ***pe*** = parenthetical expression

Each correctly placed comma is worth one point. If no commas are needed, the sentence is worth one point. Award one point for correctly underlining the interrupter and one for correctly identifying it.

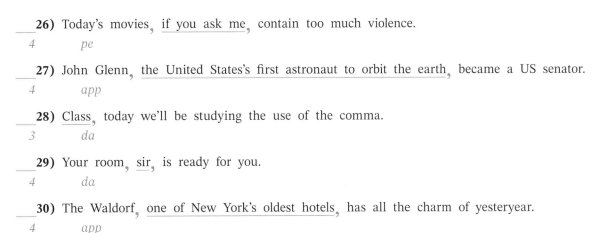

___ **26)** Today's movies, if you ask me, contain too much violence.
4   *pe*

___ **27)** John Glenn, the United States's first astronaut to orbit the earth, became a US senator.
4   *app*

___ **28)** Class, today we'll be studying the use of the comma.
3   *da*

___ **29)** Your room, sir, is ready for you.
4   *da*

___ **30)** The Waldorf, one of New York's oldest hotels, has all the charm of yesteryear.
4   *app*

_____ **31)** By the way, have you met my aunt?
  3   *pe*

_____ **32)** It is, after all, your turn to wash the dishes.
  4   *pe*

_____ **33)** Last fall I read *The Adventures of Tom Sawyer* by Mark Twain, America's foremost
  3   19th century humorist.
                app

_____ **34)** Have you seen the car keys, Mom?
  3   *da*

_____ **35)** The final game, however, was called because of rain.
  4   *pe*

  ═══
  36

Comma Rules 9, 10, and 11: Dates & Addresses, Salutations & Closings, Post-Nominal Letters

Directions

Insert commas where they are needed. Write **correct** underneath the sentence if there are no errors.

Each correctly placed comma is worth one point. If no commas are needed, the sentence is worth one point

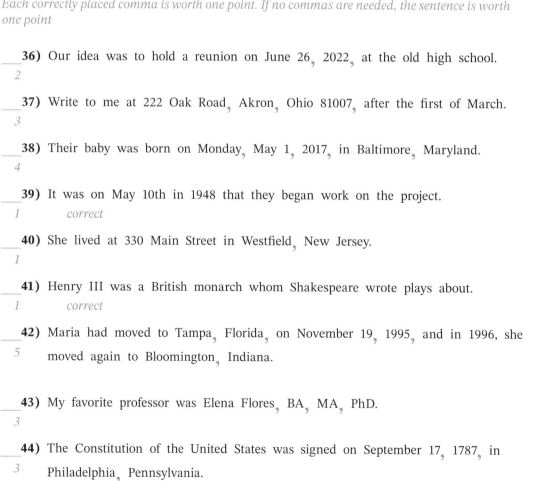

_____ **36)** Our idea was to hold a reunion on June 26, 2022, at the old high school.
  2

_____ **37)** Write to me at 222 Oak Road, Akron, Ohio 81007, after the first of March.
  3

_____ **38)** Their baby was born on Monday, May 1, 2017, in Baltimore, Maryland.
  4

_____ **39)** It was on May 10th in 1948 that they began work on the project.
  1   *correct*

_____ **40)** She lived at 330 Main Street in Westfield, New Jersey.
  1

_____ **41)** Henry III was a British monarch whom Shakespeare wrote plays about.
  1   *correct*

_____ **42)** Maria had moved to Tampa, Florida, on November 19, 1995, and in 1996, she
  5   moved again to Bloomington, Indiana.

_____ **43)** My favorite professor was Elena Flores, BA, MA, PhD.
  3

_____ **44)** The Constitution of the United States was signed on September 17, 1787, in
  3   Philadelphia, Pennsylvania.

___ **45)** Dear John,

2   Last night I heard what I thought was a cat yowling in pain outside my window. Imagine my surprise when my mother told me it was you serenading me! If you promise never to sing to me again for as long as we live, I accept your proposal of marriage!

Love and kisses,
Martha

___
25

All Comma Rules

Directions

Using all of the comma rules you have learned, insert commas where they are needed. Write **correct** underneath the sentence if there are no errors.

Each correctly placed comma is worth one point. If no commas are needed, the sentence is worth one point.

___ **46)** We left Moravia, which is a resort town in New York, and drove to Owasco Lake,
3   which is near Syracuse.

___ **47)** Michael, you know I hate tea parties, receptions, and formal dinners!
3

___ **48)** This letter is addressed to Nick Walters, Box 429, Culver City, California 90014,
5   and is dated July 14, 1991.

___ **49)** When people say I resemble my mother, I always feel flattered.
1

___ **50)** A simple, clear writing style is always appropriate.
1

___ **51)** The class studied all the comma rules in detail, and the teacher gave them a big test.
1

___ **52)** A boy riding a bicycle was seen leaving the scene of the accident.
1   *correct*

___ **53)** That dress, my dear Ms. Ames, looks beautiful on you!
2

___ **54)** Paul Bunyan, the legendary giant of the Northwest, had a blue ox for a pet.
2

___ **55)** Mrs. Hood said she isn't mad about the window and invited us in for cookies.
1   *correct*

___
20

Directions

In each sentence below, there is a comma split. All of the commas in each sentence and the spaces below them are numbered. Identify the comma split and write its number in the space next to the sentence number. In the space under each, write what it is splitting on the appropriate line. For the correctly placed commas, write the comma rule "buzzword" in the numbered space.

Correctly identifying the comma split is worth two points. Correctly completing the lines below the sentence is worth one point each.

_2_ **56)** On our trip around the country, we were really and truly, disgusted to see the litter that
_2_   1   2

    thoughtless, selfish people had dropped along the wayside.
               3

    _#1_ *introductory element*
    _1_

    _#2_ *splits linking verb* (were) *and predicate adjective* (disgusted)
    _1_

    _#3_ *two adjectives tests*
    _1_

_4_ **57)** We saw soda cans, candy wrappers, and all sorts of filthy, unsightly, garbage.
_2_   1   2   3   4

    _#1_ *items in a series*
    _1_

    _#2_ *items in a series*
    _1_

    _#3_ *two adjectives tests*
    _1_

    _#4_ *splits modifier* (unsightly) *and its noun* (garbage)
    _1_

_2_ **58)** Because of public awareness of this problem, people all over the country, are getting fed
_2_   1   2

    up with litterers, who should know better.
              3

    _#1_ *introductory element*
    _1_

    _#2_ *splits subject* (people) *and verb* (are getting)
    _1_

    _#3_ *nonessential modifiers*
    _1_

_3_ **59)** Signs, commercials, and articles have increased, our determination to do something
_2_   1   2   3

about this problem.

_1_ **#1**	*items in a series*	
_1_ **#2**	*items in a series*	
_1_ **#3**	*splits verb* (increased) *and its direct object* (determination)	

_2_ **60)** Hoping the message will get out, the media is trying to convince litterbugs to leave us,
_2_   1   2

a cleaner, more beautiful country, but we all have to help.
      3   4

_1_ **#1**	*introductory element*	
_1_ **#2**	*splits indirect object* (us) *and its direct object* (country)	
_1_ **#3**	*two adjectives tests*	
_1_ **#4**	*compound sentence*	

_27_

Total Points $\dfrac{113}{141} = 80\%$
_141_

Punctuating Quotations

Lesson 7: Punctuating Quotations

Spoken conversations and quotes make up the majority of our communication. When we are writing them down for others to read, it is important to punctuate them properly so that the reader knows which person is speaking, whether that is you as the writer, or the character or person you are writing about.

Here are a few terms that will make learning the proper punctuation easier for you:

A **direct quote** records exactly, word for word, what the speaker is saying.

> **Example:** Jackie said, "I am going to Palmer on Saturday."

> Jackie is speaking, and what she said, word for word, is
> "*I am going to Palmer on Saturday.*"

Dialogue is a conversation between two or more people.

> **Example:** Juan asked, "What are you doing this weekend, Jackie?"
> Jackie said, "I am going to Palmer on Saturday."

Again, we are quoting word for word exactly what the two speakers said. Notice that the spoken lines of dialogue in this example are direct quotes, enclosed in **quotation marks**.

Quotation marks, quote marks, or sometimes just **quotes**, are the sets of marks that come before and after a direct quote. Quotation marks always come in pairs. They look like this: "*quote goes here.*"

Narrative is the words written by the author that are not part of the spoken dialogue. In the examples above, the narrative would be *Juan asked* and *Jackie said*. Narrative refers to telling the story or relating the action during which the dialogue is happening. A narrator tells us the story, including who is saying what.

An **indirect quote** communicates what the speaker is saying, but not word for word or in first person.

> **Example:** Jackie said that she is going to Palmer on Saturday.

With an indirect quote, the writer changes the words so that they are telling the reader what was said, but not word for word. Notice that indirect quotes do not use **quotation marks**.

- Quotation marks come before and after a direct quote to enclose a person's exact words.

    Example: "We're learning about punctuation," said Joe.

    Quotation marks always come in pairs. If you **open** a quote with one quotation mark, you must **close** it with another quotation mark. Otherwise, your reader won't know where the speaker stops talking and your narration begins.

- A **direct quote** begins with a **capital letter** if the quote is a sentence.

    Example: Maria said, "The frame is not strong enough."

    If you are only quoting a portion of the speaker's words, you don't need a capital letter (or a comma—more on commas below).

    Example: Maria said that the frame "is not strong enough."

- **Broken quotes** are when a quoted sentence of dialogue is split into two parts by narrative. The beginning of the quoted sentence must begin with a capital letter, but the second part begins with a lowercase letter.

    Example: "The time has come," said Joe, "to finish my term paper."

    Joe's complete quote is, "The time has come to finish my term paper." Although it is split into two parts by narrative, *to finish my term paper* is part of the previous sentence, not a sentence on its own, and therefore, it doesn't need a capital letter.

- When you go from **narrative** to **dialogue** or from **dialogue** to **narrative**, you must use a comma to allow the reader to change gears from one to the other—unless other punctuation is already present (more on that in a minute!).

    Example: "Science is more interesting than history," said Bernie.

    Notice the comma after *history*.

    I asked, "Who is your science teacher?"

    Notice the comma after *asked*.

    "Does she let you do experiments?" asked Debbie.

    No comma is needed after *experiments* because there is already other punctuation present.

- A **comma** or a **period** is always placed **inside** the close quote mark.

    Use a **comma** if the close quote mark is not at the end of the sentence:

    Examples: "It's time to go**,**" said the guide.

    Notice that the direct quote ends with a comma because it is not at the end of the sentence. The comma is **inside** the close quote mark.

    > The man replied, "I'm ready."

    In this case, the direct quote ends with a period because it is a quoted statement at the end of the sentence. The period is **inside** the close quote mark.

- If the **dialogue** is a **question** or an **exclamation**, question marks and exclamation points should be placed **inside** the close quotes, regardless of whether the direct quote is at the beginning or end of the complete sentence. If the **narrative** is a question or an exclamation, the question mark or exclamation point should be placed **outside** of the close quote, and the direct quote does not have a comma, period, or other punctuation.

    Examples: "How far have we come?" asked the man.

    The **direct quote** is a question.

    > Who said, "Go west, young man"?

    The **narrative** is a question that includes the direct quote. The direct quote is a sentence that would normally have a period, but it does not have one because it is included in a question.

    > "Jump!" screamed the woman.

    The **direct quote** is an exclamation.

    > I nearly fainted when he said, "Time's up"!

    The **narrative** is an exclamation.

- When your direct quote consists of several sentences, place your open quotes at the beginning of the first sentence of the direct quote. Do not close the quote until the end of the entire direct quote. Place a comma, period, or other punctuation mark after the final sentence of the direct quote, according to the instructions you've already read.

    Examples: "I'm so tired. I have been working so hard on my term paper that I haven't been sleeping very well," said Alice.

    The final sentence of the direct quote is a statement. Place a comma inside the close quote.

    > "I'll wait for you at the mall. Get there as soon as you can. Try not to be late!" he said and rushed off down the hill.

    The final sentence in the direct quote is an exclamation. The exclamation mark goes inside the close quotes.

- What if the person you're quoting is quoting someone else? No need to worry—these are called **nested quotes**, or a quote within a quote. Use single quotation marks (like this: 'quote goes here') to enclose direct quotes inside direct quotes. Use the same punctuation rules for the nested quote as you do for the main quotes.

Examples: "They all yelled, 'Congratulations!' when Jack came in," Dad said.

Dad is speaking, and he is quoting what *they* yelled. Notice that, because *Congratulations!* is an exclamation, it ends with an exclamation mark **inside** the single close quote mark.

> "Did Mrs. Neumann really say, 'You may use books on the test'?" asked Sally.

Sally is asking a question, so place a question mark inside the double close quote indicating her direct quote. Sally is quoting Mrs. Neumann, who made the statement *You may use books on the test.* Because this nested quote is contained within Sally's question, and it's at the end of her direct quote, it does not need its own punctuation mark before the single close quote.

A good way to handle direct quotes is to think about them as sentences inside other sentences.

Example: 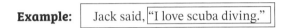 Jack said, "I love scuba diving."

The **inside** sentence is *"I love scuba diving."* I is the subject, *love* is the verb, and *scuba diving* is the direct object. Any punctuation for this sentence goes **inside** the quotation marks.

The **outside** sentence is *Jack said, "I love scuba diving."* Jack is the subject, *said* is the verb, and the quoted sentence is the direct object. Any punctuation for this sentence goes **outside** the quotation marks.

Be sure, when you're dealing with quotations, that you punctuate both the inside and outside sentences correctly!

You will never have two end marks of punctuation together unless one of them is a question mark and one is an exclamation point.

Example: "Did Jane scream, 'Help!'?" asked Mr. Bates.

Mr. Bates is asking a question, so his sentence needs a question mark. Jane is screaming, so her sentence needs an exclamation point.

> In any other situation, a question mark or exclamation point will cancel out a period or comma.

Example: "Did Jane say, 'I'm going out'?" asked Mr. Bates.

Jane's sentence, *I'm going out,* is a statement which would ordinarily end with a period. However, because Jane's sentence is inside Mr. Bates's question, the period or comma that would normally be placed before the single close quote mark is canceled out by the question mark. If Mr. Bates's direct quote were not a question, here's how it would look:

> "Jane said to me, 'I'm going out,'" said Mr. Bates.

If the direct quote comes at the end of the sentence, you will only need to use one end mark as well:

> Mr. Bates said, "Jane said to me, 'I'm going out.'"

Every open quotation mark must have a matching close quotation mark!

Other than the exclamation point/question mark situation described above, remember that you will never have a double end mark at the end of a direct quote. So, in this example, the period at the end of Jane's statement *'I'm going out'* is the only one you need. It goes inside both the single close quote and the double close quote in this case.

A note about indirect quotes:

When a direct quote is made into an indirect quote, the end punctuation mark usually becomes a period, regardless of the punctuation of the original quote. That's because the narrator is telling the reader what is being said, rather than the reader hearing it first hand. Indirect quotes are usually changed out of the first person voice, and they are not necessarily a word-for-word quote of what was said. Think of an indirect quote as a paraphrase.

Example: Direct quote: "I'm very excited to go to Wrigley Field!" shouted Nelson.
Indirect quote: Nelson shouted that he's very excited to go to Wrigley Field.

Even though Nelson was so excited that he *shouted* in his direct quote, the exclamation point is changed to a period in the indirect quote.

Example: Direct quote: "How long will it take to get there?" asked Violet.
Indirect quote: Violet asked how long it will take to get there.

Violet is still asking the question in the indirect quote, but the question mark is gone. We know it's a question because of the verb *asked*.

Punctuating Quotations: Exercise A

Directions

Rewrite the following sentences in the space provided, inserting commas, quotation marks, and capital letters where they are needed. (Make sure you don't change direct quotes to indirect quotes or vice versa!) If a sentence is correct and needs no changes, write **correct** in the space.

1) The librarian told me to be quiet.

correct

2) At the same time, Mike whispered hush up!

At the same time, Mike whispered, "Hush up!"

3) He asked can't you see that people are trying to study?

He asked, "Can't you see that people are trying to study?"

4) I replied in a whisper I'm sorry that I disturbed you.

I replied in a whisper, "I'm sorry that I disturbed you."

5) I should have known better I said to myself than to raise my voice.

"I should have known better," I said to myself, "than to raise my voice."

6) Next, I quietly asked the girl across from me for her science book.

correct

7) She whispered I'll give it to you in a minute.

She whispered, "I'll give it to you in a minute."

8) But I need it now I explained.

"But I need it now," I explained.

9) She muttered something about people who can't remember to bring their stuff.

correct

10) About that time, the bell rang and the librarian called out it's time to go, kids.

About that time, the bell rang and the librarian called out, "It's time to go, kids."

Punctuating Quotations: Exercise B

Directions

Rewrite the following sentences in the space provided, inserting proper punctuation and capitalization. Look at the clues in the sentence to determine whether you need a period, comma, question mark, or exclamation point.

Note: Unless the speaker is identified in the sentence, assume that it is a narrator speaking. That means that you don't need to put the entire sentence in quotation marks, only the direct quote.

Example: I thought I heard them say come on in.
I thought I heard them say, "Come on in."

Not: "I thought I heard them say, 'Come on in.'"

1) What do you know about the life of Mark Twain our teacher asked Lydia

"What do you know about the life of Mark Twain?" our teacher asked Lydia.

2) Did you mean it when you said I'll help you with that assignment

Did you mean it when you said, "I'll help you with that assignment"?

3) Look out screamed the man on the dock

"Look out!" screamed the man on the dock.

4) What a relief it was to hear the timekeeper say put down your pencils now
Hint: *the main sentence is an exclamation.*

What a relief it was to hear the timekeeper say, "Put down your pencils now"!

5) Do you remember asked Mrs. Bates the story of the tortoise and the hare

"Do you remember," asked Mrs. Bates, "the story of the tortoise and the hare?"

6) I leaned over and whispered are you going to be busy this afternoon

I leaned over and whispered, "Are you going to be busy this afternoon?"

7) Did anybody notice that sign that said last chance for gas for 100 miles

Did anybody notice that sign that said, **"**L*ast chance for gas for 100 miles***"?**

8) If you think shouted Bill I'm going to help you now, you're wrong

"I*f you think,***"** *shouted Bill,* **"**I*'m going to help you now, you're wrong***!"**

9) When was the last time you heard a teacher say no homework tonight, class

When was the last time you heard a teacher say, **"**N*o homework tonight, class***"?**

10) The next person who says loan me a pen is going to regret it

The next person who says, **"**L*oan me a pen,***"** *is going to regret it***!**
(a period is also correct)

Punctuating Quotations: Exercise C

Directions

Rewrite the following sentences, punctuating them correctly. Be careful—they're sneaky!

1) Noel, have you seen my catcher's mitt asked Jim it's been missing since Monday. I need it for practice today.

   "Noel, have you seen my catcher's mitt?" asked Jim. "It's been missing since Monday. I need it for practice today."

2) In what poem did Longfellow write the thoughts of youth are long, long thoughts asked Bill

   "In what poem did Longfellow write, 'The thoughts of youth are long, long thoughts'?" asked Bill.

3) Is his motto still stay in the game and pitch I asked David.

   "Is his motto still, 'Stay in the game and pitch'?" I asked David.

4) How I laughed when my science teacher referred to Bob as the young Einstein in my class exclaimed Tom

   "How I laughed when my science teacher referred to Bob as 'the young Einstein in my class'!" exclaimed Tom.

5) Did Jack shout bring my book or did he yell ring my cook asked the Duke

   "Did Jack shout, 'Bring my book!' or did he yell, 'Ring my cook!'?" asked the Duke.

Directions

If a sentence below includes an **indirect quote**, rewrite it to include a **direct quote**. If it includes a **direct quote**, rewrite it to include an **indirect quote.**

Answers will vary. Examples of possible answers are given.

6) My brother said he would miss the rehearsal.

"I'll miss the rehearsal," said my brother.

7) "What is your excuse?" asked the principal.

The principal asked him what his excuse was.

8) "Sam," asked Mia, "why aren't you playing soccer this year?"

Mia asked Sam why she wasn't playing soccer this year.

9) The thief finally admitted that he stole the jewels.

"I stole the jewels!" admitted the thief finally.

10) I told Dad I needed fifteen dollars.

"Dad, I need fifteen dollars," I said.

11) "How did you manage to get that answer?" asked the teacher.

The teacher asked how I managed to get that answer.

12) Bill yelled that the score was tied again.

"The score is tied again!" yelled Bill.

13) Grandpa said he could feel snow in the air.

"I can feel snow in the air," said Grandpa.

14) Jim said he thought he could win.

"I think I can win," said Jim.

15) "That," said Mr. Turner with a laugh, "is the first mistake I've made in ten years!"

Laughing, Mr. Turner said that it was the first mistake he'd made in ten years.

Application & Enrichment

Transitive and Intransitive Verbs

Transitive verbs are verbs which take direct objects. Can you see the word *transit* in the name? Think of transitive verbs as "transporting" the action of the verb to the direct object.

Some verbs require direct objects. Try using the verb **have** as the main verb in a sentence that doesn't have a direct object (where it is not a helping verb). It's impossible! That's because you must **have something**; you can't just **have. Have** is a transitive verb.

Intransitive verbs, then, are verbs which do not take direct objects. Try making a sentence using the verb **arrive** that has a direct object. Again, it's impossible. You don't ever **arrive something**; you just **arrive. Arrive** is an intransitive verb.

Many verbs can be transitive in some sentences and intransitive in others.

Examples: He eats lunch with me. (**eats** is transitive because it has the direct object **lunch**)

He eats with me. (**eats** is intransitive because it has no direct object)

There is a fairly small group of verbs that cause confusion for English speakers. Knowing the difference between transitive and intransitive verbs will help you choose the correct one. Three of the most commonly confused are **lay/lie, sit/set,** and **rise/raise**.

Present	Past	Past Participle
lay	laid	laid
lie	lay	lain
set	set	set
sit	sat	sat
raise	raised	raised
rise	rose	risen

To lay is a transitive verb which needs a direct object. **To lie** is intransitive and can't take a direct object.

Examples: I **lay** the book on the table. (direct object = **book**)

I **laid** the book down. (direct object = **book**)

The hen **has laid** an egg. (direct object = **egg**)

She **lies** on the sofa. (no direct object)

We **lay** in the sun. (no direct object)

He **has lain** in bed all morning. (no direct object)

To set is a transitive verb which needs a direct object. *To sit* is intransitive and can't take a direct object.

Examples: Renee **set** a record today. (direct object = *record*)
I **set** the cup on the table. (direct object = *cup*)
Have you two **set** a date yet? (direct object = *date*)

We always **sit** on the porch. (no direct object)
Joe **sat** in the third row. (no direct object)
You have **sat** in front of the TV all day. (no direct object)

To raise is a transitive verb which needs a direct object. *To rise* is intransitive and can't take a direct object.

Examples: Vern **is raising** alfalfa this year. (direct object = *alfalfa*)
He **raised** his eyebrows. (direct object = *eyebrows*)
We **have raised** our expectations. (direct object = *expectations*)

The sun **rises** in the east. (no direct object)
Al **rose** to make a speech. (no direct object)
The temperature **has risen** since noon. (no direct object)

If you are using one of these verbs in a sentence, see if you have a direct object. Then you will know which one to choose.

Directions

Circle the correct form of the verb in the sentences below.

1) The mother goose (lay, (laid)) her eggs in the tall grass.

2) The moon (raises, (rises)) in the night sky like a white balloon.

3) We ((sat,) set) in the rocking chairs on the front porch last evening.

4) Sally had (laid, (lain)) down to take a nap.

5) Winston always (raises, (rises)) to the occasion.

6) The little girl (lies, (lays)) her toy gently on the shelf.

7) Sarah has ((lain) , laid) out in the sun too long!

8) The temperature has (raised, (risen)) by at least twenty degrees.

9) We ((set,) sat) the statue carefully on its platform.

10) Josephine (rose, (raised)) teacup poodles.

11) George has (risen, (raised)) the flag every morning for ten years.

12) My grandparents love to ((sit,) set) on their front porch in the cool of the evening.

13) Try not to kill the goose that (lies, (lays)) the golden egg!

14) Has Penelope (raised, (risen)) from her "bed of pain" yet?

15) He (lay, (laid)) a bet on Knuckleduster to win the race.

Fill in the Blank

16) A(n) _____ verb takes a direct object.

transitive

17) A(n) _____ verb does not take a direct object.

intransitive

Punctuating Quotations: Assessment

Directions

Rewrite the following sentences, inserting the proper punctuation and capitalization.

Each correct capitalization and punctuation mark is worth one point.

___ **1)** did James A. Garfield really say man cannot live by bread alone he must have peanut butter

8

Did James A. Garfield really say, **"M**an cannot live by bread alone.* He must have peanut butter"?*

*Note: Students may choose to put a semicolon here, which should also be counted correct. In that case, the H should be lowercase. Don't deduct a point if they go this route; the sentence is still worth eight points if completely correct.

___ **2)** the trouble with having an open mind, of course Sir Terry Pratchett once observed is people will insist on coming along and trying to put things in it

8

"The trouble with having an open mind, of course," Sir Terry Pratchett once observed, "is that people will insist on coming along and trying to put things in it."

___ **3)** not all of us can do great things said Mother Teresa but we can do small things with great love

8

"Not all of us can do great things," said Mother Teresa, "but we can do small things with great love."

___ **4)** Mark Twain remarked it is better to remain silent and be thought a fool than to open one's mouth and remove all doubt

5

Mark Twain remarked, "It is better to remain silent and be thought a fool than to open one's mouth and remove all doubt."

___ **5)** you will face many defeats in life, but never let yourself be defeated Maya Angelou stated

5   "*You will face many defeats in life, but never let yourself be defeated,*"

Maya Angelou stated.

___ **6)** Babe Ruth advised never let the fear of striking out keep you from playing the game

5   *Babe Ruth advised,* "*Never let the fear of striking out keep you from playing the game.*"

___ **7)** life is never fair opined Oscar Wilde and perhaps it is a good thing for most of us that

8   it is not

"*Life is never fair,*" *opined Oscar Wilde,* "*and perhaps it is a good thing for most of us*

that it is not."

___ **8)** the Dalai Lama said the purpose of our lives is to be happy

6   *The Dalai Lama said,* "*The purpose of our lives is to be happy.*"

___ **9)** only a life lived for others is a life worthwhile stated Albert Einstein

5   "*Only a life lived for others is a life worthwhile,*" *stated Albert Einstein.*

___ **10)** the greatest glory in living lies not in never falling Nelson Mandela once said but in rising

8   every time we fall

"*The greatest glory in living lies not in never falling,*" *Nelson Mandela once said,* "*but in*

rising every time we fall."

____**11)** Henry David Thoreau declared go confidently in the direction of your dreams live the life

7   you've imagined

> *Henry David Thoreau declared,* "*Go confidently in the direction of your dreams!**
>
> *Live the life you've imagined.*"
>
> **A period can also be counted as correct.*

____**12)** if life were predictable mused Eleanor Roosevelt it would cease to be life and be

8   without flavor

> "*If life were predictable,*" *mused Eleanor Roosevelt,* "*it would cease to be life and be*
>
> *without flavor.*"

____**13)** Despite her trials, Anne Frank wrote whoever is happy will make others happy too

5
> *Despite her trials, Anne Frank wrote,* "*Whoever is happy will make others happy* too.*"
>
> *****Note***: Students may place a comma here. Do not count it as incorrect, nor is it worth*
> *a point.*

____**14)** you only live once Mae West claimed but if you do it right, once is enough

5
> "*You only live once,*" *Mae West claimed,* "*but if you do it right, once is enough.*"

____**15)** in the end, it's not the years in your life that count Abraham Lincoln wisely observed it's the

9   life in your years

> "*In the end, it's not the years in your life that count,*" *Abraham Lincoln wisely observed.*
>
> "*It's the life in your years.*"

103

Directions

Rewrite the following sentences, punctuating and capitalizing them properly. If the sentence is correct as written, write the word *correct*.

Each correct capitalization and punctuation mark is worth one point.

___ **16)** Did you notice Inspector Brewer asked anything peculiar about the suspect

7   "Did you notice," Inspector Brewer asked, "anything peculiar about the suspect?"

___ **17)** Just that he wore a raincoat and hid his face I replied

4   "Just that he wore a raincoat and hid his face," I replied.

___ **18)** Right said the inspector

4   "Right!*" said the inspector.
     *A comma would also be correct here.

___ **19)** I also believe he limped on his left foot I said

4   "I also believe he limped on his left foot," I said.

___ **20)** Did you say he was tall brewer asked and are you certain about the limp

8   "Did you say he was tall," Brewer asked, "and are you certain about the limp?"

___ **21)** I reminded the inspector that I had only caught a glimpse of the man.

1   correct

___ **22)** Oh, by the way I added he was carrying a small suitcase, too

7   "Oh, by the way," I added, "he was carrying a small suitcase, too."

___ **23)** Would you mind coming down to the station to make a statement Brewer asked

4   "Would you mind coming down to the station to make a statement?" Brewer asked.

___ **24)** I told him I didn't mind, but that I preferred to keep my name out of the papers.

1   correct

___ **25)** No need to worry he remarked, as he opened the squad car door for me

4   "No need to worry," he remarked, as he opened the squad car door for me.

___ **26)** I thanked him for his courtesy and got in.

1   correct

___
46

Directions

Rewrite the following sentences, punctuating and capitalizing them correctly. Be careful;
they're sneaky!

Each correct capitalization and punctuation mark is worth one point.

____ **27)** Jack asked are you sure Mr. Phillips said hand in your term papers tomorrow, class

9

Jack asked, "Are you sure Mr. Phillips said, 'Hand in your term papers tomorrow, class'?"

____ **28)** Who said I wear the chain I forged in life in Dickens's famous story asked Ms. Bailey

8

"Who said, 'I wear the chain I forged in life,' in Dickens's famous story?" asked Mrs. Bailey.

____ **29)** I always crack up when James asks what page are we on exclaimed Sue

9

"I always crack up when James asks, 'What page are we on?'!" exclaimed Sue.

$\overline{\overline{}}$
26

$\overline{\overline{}}$ *Total Points* $\quad \dfrac{140}{175} = 80\%$
175

Punctuating Dialogue

Lesson 8: Punctuating Dialogue

Now that you have practiced with the rules for punctuating quotes, punctuating dialogue should make a lot of sense.

Remember, a **dialogue** is a conversation that has two or more speakers. **Narrative** is the text that is not part of the **direct quotes**.

There are two main guidelines for writing or punctuating dialogue:

1) Start a new paragraph each time the speaker changes. The narrator, if there is one, counts as a speaker as well. Pay special attention to which narrative goes in a paragraph by itself and which goes in the same paragraph as the spoken dialogue. If the narrative tells you what one speaker is doing or thinking as well as what they are saying, put it all in the same paragraph.

Example:

"Hi," said Sean to the boy trying to open the locker next to him. "Need some help?"	Opening paragraph, with direct quote from Sean and narrative about Sean
The boy looked up. "Yeah," he said, "I'm new here and - I know this sounds dumb - but I've never had a locker before! I don't really understand how to open this thing!"	New paragraph, with direct quote from the new boy and narrative about his actions
Sean stared at the new boy. He looked like all the other kids: American accent, American clothes. How could he have gotten through junior high without having a locker? "I don't get it," said Sean. "Did you go to school on Mars?"	New paragraph, with narrative about Sean's thoughts and actions and direct quote from Sean
"You're not too far off!" laughed the boy. "My folks are with the Peace Corps in West Africa. I've never gone to school before. My mom and dad taught me at home. I feel like I really am from Mars!" He blushed and glanced at Sean uneasily. He hoped this boy, the first person who'd spoken to him in the new school, wouldn't think he was weird. He really wanted to have some friends in this new place.	New paragraph, with direct quote from the new boy and narrative about his thoughts and actions
"Gosh!" said Sean. "People are really going to make a big deal out of you! Wait'll our social studies teacher hears about this!"	New paragraph, with direct quote from Sean
The two boys walked off together down the hall, Sean asking questions as fast as he could get them out of his mouth. The new boy, Eric, was answering them the best he could, a huge grin on his face. It was going to be all right!	New paragraph, with information from the narrator about both boys' thoughts and actions. Even though this paragraph doesn't include a direct quote, it's still a new paragraph because the narrator is "speaking."

Imagine that you are a television director and that each paragraph is a camera angle. In the first paragraph above, you would have a shot of **Sean** by himself. In the next sentence, which is narrative, you would change your camera angle (or paragraph!) because it's about **Eric** and what he's doing and saying. The camera angles would go back and forth, depending on who is speaking and whose thoughts and actions are being shared. The last paragraph would require a new camera angle/paragraph because it's about what **both** boys are doing. Visualizing when a new camera angle would be needed can help you know when you need a new paragraph!

2) When a direct quote consists of more than one paragraph, put quotation marks at the ***beginning of each paragraph*** and at the ***end of the entire quote***. Do not put close quotation marks at the end of any paragraph until you reach the end of the quote.

Example: "After dinner this evening," said Denise, leaning back in her chair, "Jack and I decided to make a list of all of the jobs that need doing around here.

"We first inspected the house. The major jobs were the following: mending the hole in the sofa cushion, washing Grandma's crystal, sorting out the sheets and towels, dusting Mom's china collection, and repotting the African violets. Of course, I insisted on helping. I mean, I live here too!

"Well, I broke a crystal wine glass and a china teacup and dumped our favorite African violet out on the living room carpet. I feel like a bull in a china shop! But Jack was very kind and forgiving. He said that, in the future. I am in charge of nonbreakable jobs!" Denise concluded, smiling fondly at Jack.

Notice that each paragraph of Denise's speech begins with open quotation marks, but the close quotation marks don't appear until the very end of her entire speech.

Punctuating Dialogue: Exercise A

Directions

Rewrite the following story, using whatever paragraphing and punctuation are necessary. Remember the camera angle trick! The punctuation marks which are already included in the passage are correct.

Watch your student as they begin this exercise. At a glance, does it appear that your student understands to put the separate speakers into separate paragraphs? If it doesn't look like they've gotten the point, try dictating a few lines to them, complete with correct punctuation and paragraphs. When you get the, "oh, I see!" sign that they understand what they are doing, let them take another try.

Christmastime had finally arrived and Jim and Susan asked their parents if they could take their Christmas money out of savings to go shopping. We'll have to make a list first, said Jim. Do you think we'll have enough to buy something for everybody? asked Susan. I'm not sure, Susie, but if we don't, maybe we could go in together on some of the presents. That's a great idea, Jim! said Susan. Their parents gave them permission to get their money out of savings and drove them to the mall the next Saturday morning. Okay, said Jim. Now that we have our money, where do you want to go first? Well, why don't we try the toy store to take care of the other kids on our list? We have to be sure to buy for them. That's true, said Jim. We'll really be in trouble if we forget any of them! The two kids shopped all day. When their parents picked them up at four o'clock, two very tired youngsters climbed wearily into the car. Well, said Susan, we did it. We got something for everyone on our list. That's fantastic! said Mom. You must be really good money managers to make your money go that far! The whole family is going to be so pleased that you remembered them. Susan thought for a moment. That's true, she said glumly, which probably means that they'll get us something really nice in return. Well, you don't sound very happy about that, observed Dad. But Dad! cried Jim. Don't you understand? That means that we will have to be sure to get them something even nicer next year!

Christmastime had finally arrived and Jim and Susan asked their parents if they could take their Christmas money out of savings to go shopping.

"We'll have to make a list first," said Jim.

"Do you think we'll have enough to buy something for everybody?" asked Susan.

"I'm not sure, Susie, but if we don't, maybe we could go in together on some of the presents."

"That's a great idea, Jim!" said Susan.

Their parents gave them permission to get their money out of savings and drove them to the mall the next Saturday.

"Okay," said Jim. "Now that we have our money, where do you want to go first?"

"Well, why don't we try the toy store to take care of the other kids on our list? We have to be sure to buy for them."

"That's true," said Jim. "We'll really be in trouble if we forget any of them!"

The two kids shopped all day. When their parents picked them up at four o'clock, two very tired youngsters climbed wearily into the car.

"Well," said Susan, "We did it. We got something for everyone on our list."

"That's fantastic!" said Mom. "You must be pretty good money managers to make your money go that far! The whole family is going to be so pleased that you remembered them."

Susan thought for a moment. "That's true," she said glumly, "which probably means that they'll get us something really nice in return."

"Well, you don't sound very happy about that," observed Dad.

"But Dad!" cried Jim. "Don't you understand? That just means that we'll have to be sure to get them something even nicer next year!"

Punctuating Dialogue: Exercise B

Directions

Rewrite the following story, using whatever paragraphing and punctuation are necessary. Remember the camera angle trick! The punctuation marks which are already included in the passage are correct.

Good morning, class said Mrs. Finley. Good morning, Mrs. Finley sang the class in chorus. Today we are going to study the correct punctuation of dialogue. Yuck! said Sean. We always study the same old things said Stacy. You never show us any movies said Becky. Yeah said Jason. Mr. Johnson's class always has movies. How come we never see any movies in here? But, dear students cried Mrs. Finley. I thought you loved my class! You know how much I care! You know I just want you to be happy and have fun all the time! Don't you enjoy learning all this valuable educational material? Not really said Becky. We want to play games and read comic books and see movies shouted Chris. Yeah, who wants to be educated, anyway? said Tonya. We'd much rather be ignorant and have fun yelled Bryce. Oh, I see said Mrs. Finley. Ignorance is bliss, is that it? You got it, Mrs. Finley! Well, it grieves me deeply to see you so unhappy said Mrs. Finley but I'd really hate to see you miserable in a few short years when you hit the real world and aren't prepared! So let's get started.

"Good morning, class," said Mrs. Finley.

"Good morning, Mrs. Finley," sang the class in chorus.

"Today we are going to study the correct punctuation of dialogue."

"Yuck!" said Sean.

"We always study the same old things," said Stacy.

"You never show us any movies," said Becky.

"Yeah," said Jason. "Mr. Johnson's class always has movies. How come we never see any movies in here?"

"But, dear students!" cried Mrs. Finley. "I thought you loved my class! You know how much I care. You know I just want you to be happy and have fun all the time. Don't you enjoy learning all this valuable educational material?"

"Not really," said Becky.

"We want to play games and read comic books and see movies!" shouted Chris.

"Yeah, who wants to be educated, anyway?" said Tanya.

"We'd much rather be ignorant and have fun!" yelled Bryce.

"Oh, I see," said Mrs. Finley. "Ignorance is bliss, is that it?"

"You got it, Mrs. Finley!"

"Well, it grieves me deeply to see you so unhappy," said Mrs. Finley, "but I'd really hate to see you miserable in a few short years when you hit the real world and aren't prepared! So let's get started."

Note: This lesson has no assessment. Students will be assessed on this skill in the next lesson.

Application & Enrichment

Paraphrasing

The following is an excerpt from a poem. Parse the poem and put parentheses around the prepositional phrases. (**Hint:** don't forget BUT AL DOES!)* Then paraphrase these two stanzas.

*Refer to your notes from Level 3 on prepositional phrases if needed.

"Legacy II"

Leroy V. Quintana

       adv pro av   adv

Now I look back

       adv adj   n   v

only two generations removed

       pro   av   pp   n

who went (to college)

       v   —v— adj   n   adv

Trying to find my way back

       pp art   n   pp art   n

(to the center) (of the world)

       adv   n   av   adj   n

where Grandfather stood that day

Punctuating Titles

Lesson 9: Punctuating Titles

There are a couple of different ways we set apart titles, depending on what is being named.

Underlining or Italics

Use <u>underlining</u> (when you're handwriting or using a typewriter) or *italics* (when you're using a computer) for the titles of books, plays, movies, periodicals, works of art, podcasts, television or radio programs, long musical compositions, and albums. Parts of these larger works need quotation marks around them, shown in the next section.

The names of ships, aircraft, trains, or spacecraft should also be italicized.

Examples:

	use <u>underlining</u> if handwritten or typed	use *italics* on a computer
books	<u>Tom Sawyer</u>	*Tom Sawyer*
plays	<u>The Taming of the Shrew</u>	*The Taming of the Shrew*
movies	<u>The Blob Eats Cleveland</u>	*The Blob Eats Cleveland*
periodicals	the <u>Anchorage Times</u>	the *Anchorage Times*
works of art	the <u>Mona Lisa</u>	the *Mona Lisa*
podcasts	<u>Cattitude</u>	*Cattitude*
television programs	<u>Sesame Street</u>	*Sesame Street*
radio programs	<u>Garden Talk</u>	*Garden Talk*
long musical compositions	Beethoven's <u>Eroica</u>	Beethoven's *Eroica*
albums	<u>Meet the Beatles</u>	*Meet the Beatles*
ships	the <u>Titanic</u>	the *Titanic*
aircraft	the <u>Spirit of St. Louis</u>	the *Spirit of St. Louis*
trains	the <u>Flying Scotsman</u>	the *Flying Scotsman*
trains	the space shuttle <u>Columbia</u>	the space shuttle *Columbia*

Quotation Marks

Use quotation marks around the titles of articles, short stories, essays, poems, songs, chapters, and individual episodes of podcasts and television and radio programs. Think of it this way: Smaller works that are parts of a larger work get quotation marks.

Examples:

articles	"The Truth About OPEC"
short stories	"The Monkey's Paw"
essays	"A Modest Proposal"
poems	"The Cremation of Sam McGee"
songs	"Over the Rainbow"
chapters	"Chapter 10, The Industrial Revolution"
episodes of:	
podcasts	"Art and the Garden"—an episode of *Gardening with the RHS*
television programs	"Camp Grover"—an episode of *Sesame Street*
radio programs	"Watering the Right Way"—an episode of *Garden Talk*

One more situation in which you will need to use underlining or italics is when you are **talking about** a word, number, or letter—not using it for its meaning, but discussing it as a word. You should also use italics when you are using a word from a language other than English, if it's likely to be unfamiliar to your reader.

Examples: Does *judgment* have one or two e's?

This sentence is talking about the word *judgment* and not using its meaning of making a considered decision.

I was never happy with the way I write an *8*.

The number *8* is not referring to the quantity between *7* and *9*, but rather the figure itself.

By snatching the last taco from my future mother-in-law, I committed a terrible *faux pas.*

Notice that *taco* is not italicized in the example, because most readers are familiar with tacos. The word *faux pas* is italicized in the example because many readers may not be familiar with the term. Italicizing it sets it apart from the rest of the sentence so readers will recognize it as something different or special.

Note: If a title enclosed in quotes is used inside a direct quote, use single quotation marks as learned in Lesson 7!

Example: "Although he is best known for his novels, the short story 'The Celebrated Jumping
Frog of Calaveras County' was also written by Mark Twain," said Becca in her report.

The direct quote, beginning with *Although* and ending with *Mark Twain*, is the complete
sentence that Becca said. It is enclosed in double quotation marks. Within her sentence, she
mentions the short story "The Celebrated Jumping Frog of Calaveras County," which is enclosed
in single quotation marks because it is inside a direct quote.

The proofreading symbol that means "capitalize this letter" is a triple underline, like this:

Example: bob thompson

Punctuating Titles: Exercise A

Directions

Punctuate the following sentences correctly by inserting quotation marks and underlining where necessary.

1) Is it true that your ancestors came over on the <u>Mayflower</u>?

2) The foreign phrase <u>de rigueur</u> refers to something which is fashionable and proper.

3) Mom was completely engrossed in an article entitled "Lose Weight with Ice Cream" in this month's issue of <u>Woman's Day</u>.

4) Many jokes have been made about Rodin's magnificent sculpture <u>The Thinker</u>.

5) The quartet sang "Sweet Adeline" at the close of the program.

6) The Latin terms <u>cum laude</u>, <u>magna cum laude</u>, and <u>summa cum laude</u> usually appear on the diplomas of the best students.

7) The soprano sang the aria "One Fine Day" from the opera <u>Madama Butterfly</u>.

8) After seeing Shakespeare's <u>Julius Caesar</u>, I wrote an essay entitled "The Bard of Avon," but I was embarrassed to see that I had left out the first <u>e</u> in his name.

9) The teacher read "The Adventure of the Speckled Band" from her anthology <u>The Complete Sherlock Holmes</u>.

10) I spent my afternoon at the library reading one–hundred–year–old copies of the <u>New York Times</u>.

Punctuating Titles: Exercise B

Directions

Using all of the comma and other punctuation rules you've learned so far, properly punctuate the following sentences. Draw a triple line under all of the letters that should be capitalized.

1) The senior class play this year is <u>Arsenic and Old Lace</u>.

2) "Class, open your books to the chapter entitled 'A House Divided' in your history books," said Mrs. Mendez, holding up a copy of <u>The American Story</u>.

3) The sinking of the <u>Andrea Doria</u> in the 1950s was a terrible tragedy.

4) Billy walked proudly up to the chalkboard and spelled <u>antidisestablishmentarianism</u> with no problem!

5) Did you see the final episode of <u>The Winds of War</u> last night?

6) My mom gave me a dollar to learn to play Beethoven's "Für Elise" on the piano.

7) Mom, do you pronounce the <u>e</u> in <u>calliope</u>?

8) My subscription to <u>Newsweek</u> magazine runs out next month.

9) "I'll never forget seeing Julie Andrews in <u>My Fair Lady</u>," said Janet. "<u>M</u>my mother took me to several Broadway plays that year, but that was my favorite."

10) Edgar Allan Poe is probably best known for his poem "The Raven."

Punctuating Quotations and Titles: Exercise C

Directions

Using all of the punctuation rules you've learned so far, properly punctuate the following sentences.

1) "Nina, did you see Designing Women this week?" asked Janie. "It's my favorite TV show."

2) "The Long Search" was the most exciting chapter in the story about the lion cubs.

3) "In what poem did Longfellow write, 'the thoughts of youth are long, long thoughts'?" asked Maria.

4) "I think it was in 'My Lost Youth,'" replied Mom.

5) "Have you read 'Humor in Uniform' in the latest Reader's Digest?" asked Lee.

6) "What did Romeo mean when he said, 'It is the east, and Juliet is the sun,' in the second act of Romeo and Juliet?" asked Bill.

7) The tour group stood silently staring at the magnificence of Michelangelo's David.

8) "Sometimes when I watch Saturday Night Live, I laugh until I cry," Gracie said.

9) Pulling on the oars, the boys took the Ginger Lee out to the middle of the lake.

10) "Why doesn't anybody pronounce the r in February so a person can remember how to spell it correctly?" wailed Sharon.

Application & Enrichment

Ending a Sentence with a Preposition

Another grammar rule you may hear is this:

DO NOT END A SENTENCE WITH A PREPOSITION.

It seems straightforward, right? Here's the problem: It's wrong!

This is a rule that has been around for a very long time. In Western culture, Latin has been the language of serious academic study for centuries. When attempts were made to document the rules of English grammar, 17th century academics viewed the rules of Latin as being the best and most correct, and they tried to make English follow them. When English sentences are manipulated so that they don't end with prepositions, it results in extremely formal–sounding—and often awkward—sentences like:

> To whom do I owe the pleasure?
> That's the thing about which I am worried.
> That is the type of nonsense up with which I will not put!
>
> > – *A quote credited to Winston Churchill that is referring to this very grammar rule (although he probably didn't really say it)*

The problem is that the rules of Latin can't actually apply to English. English is not a Romance language, which is what the languages that grew out of Latin are called. French, Spanish, and Italian are Romance languages that follow Latin grammar pretty closely. In those languages, never (you'll usually find this in bold and all caps if you study these languages!), **NEVER** end a sentence with a preposition. English includes many **words** from Romance languages, but it's closest in its ***grammar*** to German, Dutch, and a little–spoken language called Frisian. Like English, it's perfectly acceptable to end sentences with prepositions in these languages.

However, many people learned this myth as a hard-and-fast rule, and it stuck. Even today there are many, many people who believe that it's incorrect to end an English sentence with a preposition. That's why, in formal writing, it's best to avoid doing it: If your reader thinks it's wrong, they may judge your writing.

- In some cases, even in informal writing, you should avoid ending sentences with a preposition— not because it breaks a rule, but because it is not necessary:

  Where are you going to?
  Where are you going?

These two sentences mean the same thing, so the preposition *to* isn't needed. Leave it out for cleaner, clearer writing.

Directions

Rewrite the sentences so that they end with a preposition. Leave out any unnecessary words.

1) Selena is the girl about whom I was telling you.

Selena is the girl I was telling you about.

2) From where did your ancestors come?

Where did your ancestors come from?

3) Our choice of restaurant depends on for what you are hungry.

Our choice of restaurant depends on what you are hungry for.

4) At Thanksgiving dinner, we list all of the things for which we are thankful.

At Thanksgiving dinner, we list all of the things we are thankful for.

5) There's nothing of which to be scared.

There's nothing to be scared of.

Directions

Rewrite the following sentences so that they do not end in prepositions. Add words if necessary.

6) Ask not whom the bell tolls for.

Ask not for whom the bell tolls.

7) What are you waiting for?

For what are you waiting?

8) Do you know whom this movie was directed by?

Do you know by whom this movie was directed?

9) We're not sure yet whose house we're staying at.

We're not sure yet at whose house we're staying.

10) The test included questions I hadn't studied for.

The test included questions for which I hadn't studied.

Punctuating Titles, Quotations, and Dialogue: Assessment

Directions

Using all of the punctuation rules you've learned so far, finish punctuating the following sentences correctly. The punctuation that is already there is correct and shouldn't be changed. Use the lesson notes if you need help.

Each correctly placed punctuation mark is worth one point.

____ **1)** Diana Ross made the song "Stop in the Name of Love" popular.
  2

____ **2)** "'The Catbird Seat' is a funny short story by James Thurber," said Tim in
  5 his oral report.

____ **3)** Did you see Jean's picture in today's Times?
  1

____ **4)** Eric had to read the book How to Eat Fried Worms for a book report.
  1

____ **5)** "The drama department is presenting The Miracle Worker for their spring play,"
  4 announced Mr. Carrera.

____ **6)** Mr. Gates assigned the fifth chapter, "Lee and His Generals," in our history book.
  4

____ **7)** Norman Lear changed television history with the series All in the Family.
  1

____ **8)** Esther used an article from Newsweek called "The Persian Gulf: What Next?" as
  4 the basis for her history report.

____ **9)** "Hey, Patty," asked Lucy, "you didn't happen to read the article 'Are You a Good
  12 Friend?' in this month's Young Miss, did you?"

____ **10)** "If you're looking for a shocking ending," said my English teacher, "you should
  9 read Shirley Jackson's short story 'The Lottery.'"
        ***Note:** close quotation marks should both be to the right of the period.*

____ **11)** "I'll never forget when my teacher read us 'An Occurrence at Owl Creek Bridge,'
  6 a famous short story," Kelly said.

____ **12)** Vincent Van Gogh's famous Sunflowers was the first painting that sold for over a
  1 million dollars.

_____**13)** Charles Lindbergh's plane was called <u>The Spirit of St. Louis</u>.
1

_____**14)** The Latin term <u>non sequitur</u> refers to a statement which is not logical.
1

_____**15)** "Mozart's comic opera <u>The Magic Flute</u> has always been a favorite of mine,"
4   said Sean.

_____**16)** "I'll never forget how embarrassed I was when I learned I had been
3   mispronouncing <u>epitome</u>. It was a big word I used all the time to try to impress

people!" laughed Kaely.

_____**17)** Dr. Gates announced, "Since you have obviously studied <u>Othello</u> so thoroughly, I
4   will assign no further reading for the weekend."

_____**18)** Jamal proudly displayed his diploma on which were the Latin words
1   <u>summa cum laude</u>, meaning "with highest honors."

_____**19)** Henry Higgins worked day and night to teach Eliza Doolittle to pronounce <u>rain</u>,
4   <u>Spain</u>, and <u>plain</u> so that the long <u>a</u> was pronounced correctly.

_____**20)** "Oh look!" exclaimed Charles as we leafed through the stack of old magazines.
7   "This 1963 issue of <u>Life</u> magazine has an article in it called 'Loch Ness

Secret Solved.'" *(or '!)*

====
75

Directions

Rewrite the following dialogue, punctuating and paragraphing correctly. The punctuation included here is correct.

21) It was a typical Saturday night at the dorm. All the guys who had dates had already gone out, but a few remained in the lounge. Hey said Jim does anybody want to go see a movie tonight? Tom, who was dozing in a huge easy chair, opened one eye. I'll go he said I'm just sitting around staring at the walls anyway. Great said Jim do you want to drive or shall I? Heaving himself out of the chair, Tom said no I'll drive. Why asked Jim. Because I don't want to be seen in that heap of yours. I have an image to protect! Jim picked up a cushion and heaved it at Tom. Trust me, pal he laughed just be seen with me and your image will be set for life! Oh yeah? Yeah! Okay said (Who is speaking here? Tom or Jim? If you paragraph correctly, you can tell!) you drive.

Sometimes the direct quotation could end with a comma, a period, or an exclamation point. As long as the rest of the punctuation and capitalization is correct for what they have chosen, give them full points.

Each new paragraph is indicated below with a blank and possible points. Each correct paragraph is worth two points. Each correct punctuation mark is worth one point.

It can be helpful to allow your student to correct their own work. Tell them how many points each paragraph is worth, and then read through it, mentioning all the paragraphing, punctuation, and capitalization. Each mistake is a one point deduction from the total possible.

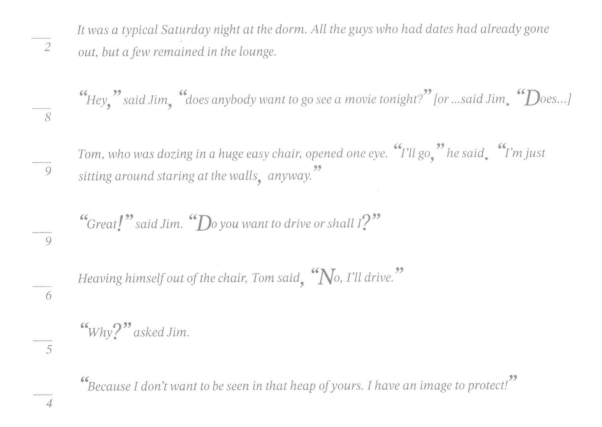

____ *It was a typical Saturday night at the dorm. All the guys who had dates had already gone*
2   *out, but a few remained in the lounge.*

____ *"Hey," said Jim, "does anybody want to go see a movie tonight?" [or ...said Jim. "Does...]*
8

____ *Tom, who was dozing in a huge easy chair, opened one eye. "I'll go," he said. "I'm just*
9   *sitting around staring at the walls, anyway."*

____ *"Great!" said Jim. "Do you want to drive or shall I?"*
9

____ *Heaving himself out of the chair, Tom said, "No, I'll drive."*
6

____ *"Why?" asked Jim.*
5

____ *"Because I don't want to be seen in that heap of yours. I have an image to protect!"*
4

___
9

Jim picked up a cushion and heaved it at Tom. "Trust me, pal!" *he laughed.* "Just be seen with me and your image will be set for life!"

or

"Trust me, pal," *he laughed,* "just be seen with me and your image will be set for life!"

___
4

"Oh yeah?"

___
4

"Yeah!"

___
10

"Okay," *said* Tom, "you drive."

___
70

=== *Total Points* $\dfrac{116}{145} = 80\%$
145

Semicolons and Colons

Lesson 10: Semicolons and Colons

Like commas, semicolons and colons are used to insert pauses into the flow of sentences. These punctuation marks are frequently used incorrectly because they are seen as just bigger and better commas—they are not! There are some very specific situations in which they should be used. Using them correctly makes your writing appear more polished and credible.

Use semicolons (;) when:

Joining independent clauses

The most common correct use of a semicolon is between independent clauses (sentences) **if they are not joined by a conjunction**. Remember those comma splices from Lesson 1? Those writers could have used a semicolon!

> **Example:** Mary enjoys fantasy novels; her brother likes mysteries.

On either side of the semicolon is an independent clause, which could stand alone as a sentence. The semicolon signals to the reader that more is coming; the thought in the first clause was not quite finished, and it is completed in the clause after the semicolon.

Using a transitional device

Use a semicolon between independent clauses joined by such words as *for example, for instance, therefore, that is, besides, accordingly, moreover, nonetheless, furthermore, otherwise, however, consequently, instead, hence*. The semicolon should be placed before the transitional word or phrase.

These words are called **transitional devices** because they help the reader make the transition from one thought to another. They are very useful when a writer is trying to show the relationship between one idea and another. Transitional devices are an **introductory element** and should be set apart from the rest of the sentence with a **comma**.

> **Example:** Jane showed me in many ways that she was still my friend. She saved me a seat on the bus.

It's a bit difficult to see the relationship between these two sentences. However, with a transitional device, we have:

> Jane showed me in many ways that she was still my friend; *for example*, she saved me a seat on the bus.

With the addition of *for example*, we understand that the writer is giving the fact that Jane saved them a seat on the bus as evidence that she was still their friend.

You can (and should!) use transitional devices without using a semicolon, too; however, **with** the semicolon, the ideas presented in the two independent clauses are more closely related in the reader's mind. The use of transitional devices, even without a semicolon, tells the reader that the writer is presenting additional information about, or possibly that contrasts with, the topic of the first sentence.

Separating the independent clauses of a compound sentence (sometimes)

Ordinarily, two sentences joined by a conjunction will only need a comma to separate them. But if the independent clauses have commas in them already, using a semicolon can help the reader if there might be confusion where one sentence ends and the second sentence begins.

> **Example:** She will invite Elaine, Kim, and Stacey, and Val will ask Molly.

Confusing! The two independent clauses/sentences in this compound sentence are *She will invite Elaine, Kim, and Stacey* and *Val will ask Molly.* We know that items in a series need commas between them and before the conjunction and final item, so we're clear in the example sentence until we get to *...and Stacey, and...* Wait. With the comma and conjunction, we know that we are wrapping up our list of items...but then there's another comma and another *and!*

At first read, we stumble because we initially think *She* is going to invite *Elaine* and *Kim* and *Stacey* **and** *Val*, but *she* isn't.

A clearer way to punctuate this sentence is to use a semicolon instead of a comma before the conjunction joining the two sentences:

> She will invite Elaine, Kim, and Stacey; and Val will ask Molly.

Much clearer! The semicolon after *Stacey* signals to the reader, "The previous thought is complete; this is a new thought."

Separating items in a series (sometimes)

Like compound sentences, items in a series usually only need commas to separate them. If your list items already include commas for another reason, however, use a semicolon to separate them.

Example: The dates of the testing are Monday, April 4, Tuesday, April 5, and Wednesday, April 6.

Confusing! Those are a lot of commas for the reader to try to process.

> The dates of the testing are Monday, April 4; Tuesday, April 5; and Wednesday, April 6.

Much clearer!

Remember that the goal of punctuation is to guide a reader through written communication. Using a semicolon where necessary is very helpful for them to know what a sentence is communicating.

Use colons (:) to:
Indicate "note what follows"

A colon should be used before a list of items, especially after an expression like *as follows* or *the following.* The words **before** the colon must be a complete sentence. A colon should never split a sentence.

Example: You will need to take the following things: a heavy jacket, boots, a sleeping bag, a hunting knife, and a backpack.

Note that your list items should be punctuated as any other items in a series, with commas (or semicolons) between each item, including the final conjunction and item.

> I have three extracurricular activities: reading, skiing, and playing video games.

If a list follows an otherwise complete sentence, use a colon even if there's no expression indicating that a list is coming.

> We traveled to three cities in Europe: Barcelona, Spain; Hamburg, Germany; and Naples, Italy.

This list uses semicolons between items because the items themselves include commas.

Incorrect colon use:

> **Examples:** My extracurricular activities are: reading, skiing, and playing video games.

> The phrase before the colon is not a complete sentence. The colon splits the helping verb (*are*) and its predicate nominatives (*reading*, etc.). The colon should be **left out** of this sentence.

> Mix the sifted flour with: cinnamon, nutmeg, ginger, and sugar.

> The phrase before the colon is not a complete sentence. The colon splits the preposition (*with*) and its objects (*cinnamon*, etc.). The colon should be **left out** of this sentence.

Set apart a long quote

If you are quoting someone else's work and the narrative used to introduce the quotation is a complete sentence including more information than *The speaker said*, use a colon to set the quotation apart from the narrative. Particularly if the quotation is longer than a single sentence, use a colon. You should still enclose the quotation in quotation marks.

> **Example:** Horace Mann had this to say about dealing with those who disagree with you: "Do not think of knocking out another person's brains because he differs in opinion from you. It would be as rational to knock yourself on the head because you differ from yourself ten years ago."

> The introductory sentence provides information to give context to the quote. The writer is emphasizing that the quotation concerns *those who disagree with you*. Compare that to the following:

> Horace Mann said, "Do not think of..."

In this instance, the only information provided in the introductory clause is that the speaker said something. When including direct quotations in your writing, consider using a complete introductory sentence in the narrative to guide your reader to focus on the point you wish to make.

> If what follows the colon is a complete sentence/independent clause, capitalize it!

Punctuate specific items
- Between the hour and minute when you write the time (7:30, 8:46, and so on)

- Between the chapter and verse when referring to passages from the Bible, the Quran, or other books organized in this manner (Genesis 2:2, Quran 64:3)

- After the salutation of a business letter (Dear Sir:)

> For these exercises, you may be **editing**. When you edit, you correct any mistakes you find in sentences. There are certain symbols that editors use. One of them is the "delete" symbol. Use this symbol to delete commas, other punctuation, words, or even entire paragraphs from written work.

> The symbol looks like this: ♂

Semicolons and Colons: Exercise A

Directions

Some of the sentences below require semicolons or commas, some have semicolons that should not be there, some have semicolons that should be commas, and some of the sentences are correct. Put in the missing semicolons and commas, cross out and correct the errors, or write **correct** after the sentences that are correct as written. Use the lesson notes from this and other punctuation lessons if you need help.

1) Many people feel insecure about punctuation; they never know whether they're right or wrong!

2) In ancient times, writers didn't use punctuation; therefore, their writings are difficult to read.

3) As a matter of fact, writers during the days of ancient Greece and Rome didn't even put a space between each word!
   correct

4) Life moved at a much slower pace than it does today; hence, it wasn't that important to be able to read something quickly.

5) The ability to read and write was a rare one; consequently, few people depended on the written word as we do today.

6) Most people lived their entire lives without ever sending or receiving a letter; they didn't need to know how to read and write.

7) Although people honored and respected those who could read; , they didn't see the need for it in their own lives.

8) Toward the latter part of the Middle Ages, nations began to trade widely with each other; literacy became a necessity for success in business.
   correct

9) A merchant could expect to receive several written messages in a day; it became important to be able to read something quickly.

10) Earlier in ancient times, some smart writer figured out that if he left a space between words, his writing could be read more quickly; we're all grateful to this obscure writer!

11) There has to be something to tell us when a sentence ends; otherwise, we might think that the end of one sentence is the beginning of the next.

12) Somewhere along the line, a writer decided to put a dot at the end of each sentence; this made writing much clearer.

13) In time, other "end marks" of punctuation appeared; one of these is the question mark.
   correct

14) When these writers used certain marks, they found it easier to convey their true meaning; other people saw the value of it and simply copied what the other guy did!

15) Eventually, writers began to use many punctuation marks; therefore, it became necessary to agree upon some rules.

16) In the early days, punctuation was free-wheeling; Shakespeare used it pretty much as he pleased!

17) Commas began to be used in a more orderly way; for example, commas were used to separate items in a series.

18) Other situations in which a comma became necessary were appositives, which are groups of words that restate other nouns; nonessential modifiers, which are word groups used to modify nouns; and direct address, which is a word or words used to refer to the person one is speaking to.

19) Everybody should learn how to punctuate correctly; otherwise, other people will have a hard time understanding their writing.

20) So next time you get tired of learning these punctuation rules, remember what punctuation is really for; it helps us all communicate more quickly and clearly!

Semicolons and Colons: Exercise B

Directions

Decide where colons should appear in the following sentences and write them in. Write ***correct*** after any sentences that are correct as written.

1) In science class, we have to learn the meanings of the following words: amphibian, chromosome, neutron, oxidation, and vertebrae.

2) Miss Thompson invited Bryant, Javy, and Tony.
correct

3) The farmer explained the uses of the various parts of the plow: landslide, clevis, jointer, and beam.

4) Experts can identify a fingerprint by observing the nature of the following: arches, whorls, loops, and composites.

5) At 10:45, the teacher rang the bell to end the lesson.

6) At 8:20, the agent told us that the 6:10 train would not arrive before 9:15.

7) Along the midway were several kinds of rides: a roller coaster, a ship, two merry-go-rounds, and a Ferris wheel.

8) There were sandwiches, cold drinks, and candy on our trays.
correct

9) At an airport, I like to listen to the many noises: motors roaring before takeoff, loudspeakers announcing departures and arrivals, and telephones ringing at every counter.

Semicolons and Colons: Exercise C

Directions

Some of the sentences below require semicolons, colons, or commas; some have semicolons that should not be there; some have semicolons that should be commas; and some of the sentences are correct. Put in the missing semicolons, colons, or commas; cross out and correct the errors; or write *correct* after the sentences that are correct as written. Use the lesson notes from this and other punctuation lessons if you need help.

1) A scrawny, friendly stray dog wandered onto the field; the umpire stopped the game.

2) Because they do not conduct electricity, the following materials can be used as insulators: rubber, glass, cloth, and plastic.

3) There are only three primary colors: red, yellow, and blue.

4) Other colors are mixtures of primary colors; for example, purple is a mixture of red and blue.

5) The cowboy's ten-gallon hat was used as a protection from the sun, a dipper for water, and a pan for washing his hands; and his leather chaps protected him from thorny bushes.

6) The pastor began her sermon by quoting these two verses from the Bible: Matthew 23:30 and John 16:27.

7) In his speech to the Thespian Society, Mr. Chen quoted from several Shakespearean plays: *Romeo and Juliet*, *The Tempest*, *Macbeth*, and *Julius Caesar.*

8) Captain James Cook explored much of the Pacific Ocean; he reached Hawaii in 1778.

9) From 1851 to 1864, the United States had four presidents: Millard Fillmore, a Whig from New York; Franklin Pierce, a Democrat from New Hampshire; James Buchanan, a Democrat from Pennsylvania; and Abraham Lincoln, a Republican from Illinois.

10) From 1:15 to 1:50 this afternoon, I was so sleepy that my mind wandered; I rested my head on my right palm and let my eyelids sag to half-mast.

Application & Enrichment

Phrasal Adjectives and Hyphens

We've learned that adjectives are words that modify, or describe, nouns. We also know that adverbs modify adjectives (among other things). There are some situations, however, in which the two parts of speech work together to create a **phrasal adjective**. Phrasal adjectives can also be created by combining a noun or an adverb with an adjective to make another adjective. Like all adjective phrases, these two (or more) words combine to make a phrase that acts as a single modifier. This is different from using multiple adjectives that can stand on their own.

To show that the phrasal adjective should be viewed as one unit, and to avoid confusion, it is usually hyphenated. If the two parts of the hyphenated word were simply regular adjectives, they would be separated by a comma. You could change the order without changing the meaning of the phrase. Both adjectives could independently modify the noun, and it would still make sense.

Regular adjectives	large, brown chickens	tall, beautiful tree
Separated	large chickens brown chickens	beautiful tree tall tree
Reversed order	brown, large chickens	beautiful, tall tree

These make sense separately and mean the same thing when reversed.

In a hyphenated phrasal adjective, the hyphen can't be removed because the two parts of the phrasal adjective need to be connected in a specific order to provide the intended meaning.

Phrasal adjective	free-range hens	part-time employees	five-second rule
Separated	free hens range hens	part employees time employees	five rule second rule
Reversed order	range, free hens	time, part employees	second five rule

These don't mean the same thing as the original when separated or reversed.

A phrasal adjective can have more than two words:

> three-year-old child

> 24-hour-a-day supervision

Sometimes leaving out the hyphen can change the meaning even if the parts of the phrasal adjective are in the correct order. The hyphen tells the reader's mind which words to group together:

> disease-causing germs (The germs cause the disease.)

> disease causing germs (The disease causes the germs.)

Using a hyphen can have the opposite meaning from not using one.

Directions

Find the phrasal adjectives in the sentences below and circle them. Then rewrite them correctly.

1) The (small business) owner joined the local Chamber of Commerce.

small-business

2) My dog is not a (full blooded) husky, but he is just as stubborn as one!

full-blooded

3) A company wants to build a (four story) building next to my aunt's house.

four-story

4) Juliana sent emails to (old book) retailers to find an original copy of Jane Austen's *Emma.*

old-book

5) Envy is known as the "(green eyed) monster."

green-eyed

6) Our teacher said our projects would be graded on a (first come, first served) basis.

first-come, first-served

7) The (six month old) baby was laughing happily at her big brother.

six-month-old

8) Singing "Take Me Out to the Ballgame" is a (time honored) tradition at Wrigley Field.

time-honored

9) The (cold blooded) reptile loved to sit on a heated rock in the sun.

cold-blooded

10) In knitting, dropping a stitch is an (all too common) mistake.

all-too-common

Semicolons and Colons: Assessment

Directions

Insert semicolons where they are needed. You may need to change some commas to semicolons.

Each correctly punctuated sentence is worth one point.

____ **1)** Take Mom's suitcase upstairs, please; you can leave Dad's in the car for now.
1

____ **2)** I wrote to Anna, Beth, and Meghan; and Juan notified Ted and Violet.
1

____ **3)** The Stone of Scone was used in ancient Scottish coronations; it lay for years
1 beneath the coronation chair in Westminster Abbey.

____ **4)** Alaska is untamed and wild; it is also modern and sophisticated.
1

____ **5)** Dad threw the coat away; it was worn out.
1

____ **6)** Janet did as she was told; however, she grumbled ungraciously.
1

____ **7)** From 1968 to 1988, the presidents of the United States were Richard Nixon,
3 a Republican from California; Gerald Ford, a Republican from Michigan;
Jimmy Carter, a Democrat from Georgia; and Ronald Reagan, a Republican
from California.

____ **8)** Mr. Baxter, who never raised his voice in the classroom, began to shout; obviously,
1 he had been pushed beyond his limit.

____ **9)** After the fire, the family stood in the smoke-blackened dining room; the house, now
1 a smoking shell, no longer looked like their own.

____ **10)** Never be afraid to admit that you don't know something; always be embarrassed to
1 admit that you don't want to learn.

12

Directions

Some of the sentences below need colons; insert them where needed. Some of them have colons that should not be there; cross those out. Some of them are correct: write **correct** below them.

____ **11)** A search showed that Jack's pocket contained the following: a knife, half an apple,
1　　　a piece of gum, a dime, and a nickel.

____ **12)** These cookies are made of: flour, brown sugar, butter, eggs, and nuts.
1

____ **13)** At the drugstore, I bought a comb, a lipstick, and a box of tissues.
1　　*correct*

____ **14)** The following students should report to the main office: Anne Brown, Pete Herdez,
1　　　Mary Jo Derum, and Lana Williams.
　　　correct

____ **15)** I have always wanted to do three things: climb a mountain, ride a racehorse, and
1　　　take a hot air balloon ride.

____ **16)** We have studied the following kinds of punctuation marks: commas, quotation
1　　　marks, colons, and semicolons.
　　　correct

____ **17)** To succeed in sports, one should be disciplined, coordinated, and motivated.
1　　*correct*

____ **18)** You need these supplies for this class: white, lined notebook paper; a blue or black
1　　　pen; and a pencil.

____ **19)** At exactly 3:15, we will begin our meeting.
1

――
9

Directions

Using all of the punctuation marks we have learned so far, properly punctuate the following sentences. Use the lesson notes if you need help.

Each punctuation mark correctly provided or deleted is worth one point.

____ **20)** One of my favorite cowboy movies is called 3:10 to Yuma; it's about a law
3
officer who must get his prisoner onto the train that leaves for Yuma at ten

minutes after three.

____ **21)** "Lightning has always awed people," explained Mrs. Belmont, "and many of us
7
are still frightened by it."

____ **22)** "Have you read Poe's short story 'The Pit and the Pendulum?'" asked Jenna.
4

____ **23)** "You'll need the following materials for this art course: a brush, an easel, and
6
some watercolors," announced Mr. Greene.

____ **24)** "Have you seen this month's issue of Seventeen?" asked Gloria.
4

____ **25)** At 8:15 on March 1, 1980, we ate the last of our provisions.
3

____ **26)** We thought we were taking a short cruise; however, it turned out to be
2
quite a long trip.

____ **27)** Robert Burns, a Scottish poet, wrote the poem "Flow Gently, Sweet Afton."
4

____ **28)** In the novel Little Women, there are four sisters: Meg, Jo, Beth, and Amy.
6

____ **29)** "Sally, who is my older sister, is coming home from college tonight,"
5
announced Jerome.

____ **30)** Lenore was a poised, self-confident young woman; her ambition was to get
2
involved in local politics.

___**31)** The finalists in the Miss Stuffed Artichoke contest were Pearl Button,
8
a stunning blond from West Mudsling, Wisconsin; Ima Sweethart, a dainty

brunette from Gnaw Bone, Indiana; and Reina Ponderoof, a pretty redhead

from Lower Intestine, Nevada.

___**32)** My brothers and sisters have these characteristics in common: kindness,
3
unselfishness, and loyalty.

___**33)** Opening his copy of the <u>Wall Street Journal</u>, Dad settled back in his chair and
6
announced, "I do not wish to be disturbed; I have had a difficult day."

___**34)** "Open your books, but don't start yet," said Miss Ames, my math teacher.
5

___**35)** The members of the senior class, who had been working very hard, had a great
5
time at the Prom; and the Winter Ball, which was put on by the juniors, was also

a big success.

___**36)** Professor Hensley, hurrying down the corridor with his nose buried in Steinbeck's
5
great novel <u>The Grapes of Wrath</u>, bumped right into Miss Peabody, the tall,

muscular physical education teacher.

___**37)** "Since I had planned to stay home and watch <u>Saturday Night Live</u>, I decided to
6
make some popcorn; that was my first mistake," explained Gail.

___**38)** "The next morning, one of the crew shouted, 'Land ho!'" said Jim.
6

$$\overline{\overline{90}}$$

$$\overline{\overline{\underset{111}{}}} \; Total \; Points \quad \frac{89}{111} = 80\%$$

Forming the Possesive

Lesson 11: Forming the Possessive

When we want to indicate that something belongs to or is owned by someone or something, we use a **possessive adjective**. The possessive is formed by adding either **'** or **'s** to a noun. The possessive adjective and its noun together form a **possessive phrase**. It can be helpful to "flip" the possessive phrase to identify it.

To form the possessive of

- a **singular noun**, add **'s**.

  - woman's dress - the dress of the woman

  - baby's toys - the toys of the baby

  - octopus's garden - the garden of the octopus

  - Gus's book - the book belonging to Gus

- a **plural noun ending in s**, add **'**.

  - cats' fur - the fur of the cats

  - girls' soccer team - the soccer team of the girls

  - two weeks' notice - notice of two weeks

  - puppies' chew toys - the chew toys belonging to the puppies

- a **plural noun not ending in s**, add **'s**.

  - men's locker room - the locker room of the men

  - sheep's fleeces - the fleeces belonging to the sheep

  - people's occupations - the occupations of the people

  - oxen's harnesses - the harnesses of the oxen

Some words already show possession without needing any changes. These words don't need apostrophes or an added **s**. They are called **possessive pronouns**, and we were introduced to them way back in Level 3.

Possessive Pronouns

Possessive pronouns take the place of the possessive adjective in the possessive phrase.

Examples: Maria's convertible - the convertible belonging to *Maria*
her convertible - the convertible belong to *her*

the people's court - the court belonging to *the people*
their court - the court belonging to *them*

Some possessive pronouns are able to stand alone to take the place of the entire possessive phrase.

Little Bo Peep has lost *her sheep*.
Little Bo Peep has lost *hers*.

They'll come home, wagging *their tails* behind them.
They'll come home, wagging *theirs* behind them.

The number and gender should be matched to the possessive adjective being replaced.

Possessive Pronouns	Stand-Alone Possessive Pronouns	Belonging to:
my	mine	me
your	yours	you
his	his	him
her	hers	her
its	its	it
our	ours	us
their	theirs	them

Possessive pronouns never have apostrophes. They are possessive by nature and don't need to have *'s* added or to change in any way to show possession. Remember that with pronouns, apostrophes show contractions and **not** possession!

A Special Note about *Its* and *It's*

It's easy to learn to recognize that *our's* and *her's* are incorrect—neither of them are actually words. We can memorize that *ours* and *hers* and the other possessive pronouns never have apostrophes. That way, when we see them spelled with one, we know right away that they're wrong. But what about *it's* and *its*? These two can be tricky, because they are both really words!

To know what to do with *it's* and *its*, consider what you are trying to say. If you want to show that *it* is in possession of something, you will use the possessive pronoun *its*.

> **Example:** The kitten has lost the kitten's mittens. (*The kitten has lost the mittens belonging to **it**.*)
>
> The kitten has lost *its* mittens. (no apostrophe needed, because *its* is a possessive pronoun)

It's, on the other hand, is a contraction of the words *it is*. It needs an apostrophe to show that there is a letter missing.

> The *kitten* is going to look for them.
> *It is* going to look for them.
> *It's* going to look for them.

If you want to use either *its* or *it's*, and you're not sure which is correct, see if your sentence makes sense if you substitute *it is* in the place where you want to say *its* or *it's*. If it does, great! Go ahead and use *it's*. If it doesn't, though, you need to use the possessive pronoun *its*.

To be sure how to properly form the possessive adjective, it's important to identify whether it is a singular or plural noun. Use other clues from the sentence or paragraph to help you know how to punctuate the possessive adjective.

> **Example:** The *girls basketball team* won their game.

In the sentence, *girls* is a plural noun. We can tell because we see that *their* is used to refer to the girls later in the sentence. For a plural noun ending in *s*, just add an apostrophe.

> The *girls' basketball team* won their game.

The *girls heart* was filled with joy because she scored the winning basket!

In this sentence, *girl* is a singular noun; we know this because the pronoun *she* is used to describe her later in the sentence. For singular nouns, add *'s*:

The *girl's heart* was filled with joy because she scored the winning basket!

Never try to make the plural form of a word by adding *'s!* *'s* is only used to form possessive adjectives or contractions with the word *is* in them. If a singular noun ends in *-s* (or in letters that make an *s* or *z* sound, for example), add *-es* to make it plural.

Examples:

Singular	Correct Plural	Incorrect Plural
glass	glasses	glass's
Mr. Stephens	the Stephenses	the Stephens'
one audio CD	two audio CDs	two audio CD's

The **only exception to this rule** is when you are talking about individual letters of the alphabet and you could cause confusion by just adding an *s*.

Example: It is difficult to tell his *es* from his *ls* when he writes.
It is difficult to tell his *e's* from his *l's* when he writes.

In the first sentence, even with the italics for *e* and *l*, it's confusing at first read. The apostrophes help the reader know that the single letters are what's intended.

Possessives: Exercise A

Directions

Use clues from the sentence to properly punctuate the possessive adjective. All of the possessive adjectives in this section already have the required **s** added. You will need to determine where the apostrophe should be placed. You may need to use your detective skills to identify which word is being modified! Next, "flip" the possessive phrase you have created and write it as shown in the example.

Example: The boys' basketball team plays tonight.
the basketball team of the boys

1) Tom's team won the game.

   the team of Tom

2) The girls' soccer tryouts will be next week.

   soccer for girls (or soccer tryouts for the girls)
   *(**Note:** This could also be punctuated as girl's, if the argument is made that there is only one girl.)*

3) I sell men's clothing in my store.

   clothing for men

4) The store next door sells children's toys.

   toys for children

5) Mr. Herrera is in the teachers' lounge.

   lounge of the teachers

6) The swimming pool's gate is locked.

   gate of the swimming pool

7) Pumpkin's food dish is empty.

   food dish of Pumpkin

Directions

Properly punctuate the possessive adjectives in the following sentences. Flip the possessive phrase in your head or use the lesson notes if you need help determining where the apostrophe should be placed.

8) Bonnie's team won the quiz bowl.

9) Micah's little sister got lost in the store.

10) My two brothers' clothes were all over the floor.

11) That girl's book fell out of the car.

12) The doctor gently felt the dog's paw.

13) I left my sweater at the dentist's office.

14) Sammy's hobby is collecting ballplayers' autographs.
    (This sentence has two possessive adjectives!)

Directions

The possessive phrases in the following sentences have been "flipped." Rewrite each sentence to include a possessive adjective with the proper punctuation.

Example: The dog of the man met him joyfully at the door.

The man's dog met him joyfully at the door.

15) The hat of that tall man blew down the street.

That tall man's hat blew down the street.

16) There are the coats of two girls in the closet.

There are two girls' coats in the closet.

17) We found the bike which belongs to Ramon in the basement.

We found Ramon's bike in the basement.

18) It was The Day for Veterans at Yankee Stadium.

It was Veterans' Day at Yankee Stadium.

Possessives: Exercise B

Directions

Correctly form the possessive adjectives in the following sentences. Use the lesson notes to help you. Flip the possessive phrase if that is helpful. Be careful, as there may be more than one possessive adjective in a sentence.

1) The children's presents are in the hall closet.

2) Anna's store sells maps and travel books.

3) Ross's golf bag is in my father's car.

4) That architect's designs have won many awards.

5) Many campers' tents were destroyed by the windstorm.

6) We used Trish's scarf as a bandage.

7) Louis's phone number has been changed.

8) The boys' basketball team was undefeated.

9) Tess's butterfly collection has two dozen specimens.

10) The sailors' raincoats protected them from the spray.

Directions

The possessive phrases in the following sentences have been "flipped." Rewrite each sentence to include a possessive adjective with the proper punctuation.

11) The library for children closes at five o'clock.

   The children's library closes at five o'clock.

12) We found the mittens of George.

   We found George's mittens.

13) Which department sells cribs for babies?

   Which department sells babies' cribs?

14) Where are the tickets of the women?

   Where are the women's tickets?

15) The house of George Jones is on this street.

   George Jones's house is on this street.

16) The house of the Joneses is on this street.

   The Joneses' house is on this street.

17) I will be with you again in the time of two days.

   I will be with you again in two days' time.

18) I can only take a vacation of one week this year.

I can only take one week's vacation this year.

19) Please give me the worth of two dollars in quarters.

Please give me two dollars' worth of quarters.

20) The teachings of Socrates are still studied today.

Socrates's teachings are still studied today.

Directions

Write the words according to the following directions.

Word	Possessive	Plural	Plural Possessive
lady	*lady's*	*ladies*	*ladies'*
child	*child's*	*children*	*children's*
man	*man's*	*men*	*men's*
girl	*girl's*	*girls*	*girls'*
woman	*woman's*	*women*	*women's*

Possessives: Exercise C

Directions

Write the words according to the following directions.

Word	Possessive	Plural	Plural Possessive
baby	*baby's*	*babies*	*babies'*
sheep	*sheep's*	*sheep*	*sheep's*
Tom Smith	*Tom Smith's*	*The Smiths*	*The Smiths'*
mouse	*mouse's*	*mice*	*mice's*
boy	*boy's*	*boys*	*boys'*

Directions

Place apostrophes in the proper places in the sentences below.

1) The governor's mansion was lit by floodlights.

2) Three policemen's uniforms were in the back of the car.

3) My aunt's favorite color is magenta.

4) We need a stretcher to carry the team's mascot to the locker room.

5) Juan took three weeks' vacation to Tahiti this year.

6) Please give me two dollars' worth of change.

7) Let's go to the old swimming hole for old times' sake.

8) Julie's skirt was shorter than hers.

9) In college we studied Aristophanes's speeches.

10) Coach Gillis's daughter is coming to the game this week.

Directions

Rewrite the following sentences using possessive adjectives.

11) Tonight we are having dinner at the house of the Finleys.

Tonight we are having dinner at the Finleys' house.

12) Janie suddenly realized that she was in the locker room for the boys.

Janie suddenly realized that she was in the boys' locker room.

13) I asked for the worth of a dollar in change.

I asked for a dollar's worth of change.

14) I said I would see him in the time of two months.

I said I would see him in two months' time.

15) After the study of four years, I considered myself an expert in economics.

After four years' study, I considered myself an expert in economics.

Directions

On a separate piece of paper, make the following nouns into possessive adjectives and create your own sentences.

Answers will vary, but possessive should look like this:

16) Sally

Sally's

17) Socrates

Socrates's

18) any singular noun

varies

19) Ross

Ross's

20) any plural noun not ending in -s

varies

Application & Enrichment

Phrasal Adjectives: When *Not* to Hyphenate

In the previous Application & Enrichment activity, you learned about hyphenating phrasal adjectives to make the meaning clearer to readers. In many cases, a hyphen is helpful to tie together modifiers that act as one adjective. Sometimes, however, a hyphen should not be used:

- When one of the modifiers is an adverb ending in *-ly*:

  a commonly used phrase
  an amazingly long walk
  a terribly hot day

  Many readers, perhaps unconsciously, recognize that *-ly* signals a modifier and that what follows is the word it is modifying. No hyphen is needed.

- When the modifier includes proper names or foreign phrases:

  a Guggenheim Museum exhibit (*not* a Guggenheim-Museum exhibit)

- When the phrasal adjective comes after the noun:
  In both of these sentences, *face* is being modified by the same phrasal adjective. The first one needs hyphens; the second doesn't.

  Her hard-to-place face gave me no clues about where I had met her. (*hyphens*)
  I knew I had met her, but her face was hard to place. (*no hyphens*)

In other cases, you may not *need* a hyphen. When the phrasal adjective is frequently used as a compound noun, hyphens are not necessary:

  The high school classes were more difficult than the junior high classes.

High school and *junior high are* compound nouns that are easily recognized by most people as compound nouns, so you do not have to use hyphens.

If there is any possibility that your readers may be confused by a phrasal adjective and its noun, use hyphens!

Look at what you have written. Is there any possibility that the reader could be confused?

  The bank offers a big business loan. (*a business loan for a lot of money*)
  The bank offers a big-business loan (*a loan for big businesses*)

  The small animal veterinarian opened their new office.
  (*The veterinarian is a small animal.*)
  The small-animal veterinarian opened their new office.
  (*The veterinarian treats small animals.*)

Remember that the purpose of punctuation is to make written communication more easily understood by readers. Anything that causes them to pause or stumble in their reading is an opportunity to lose their interest. Modern grammar experts agree that if adding a hyphen helps even one reader who would have otherwise been confused, then you should use one.

Directions

Circle the phrasal adjective(s) in each sentence. Decide whether each one needs a hyphen or not.

- If it **doesn't have** a hyphen but **should be hyphenated**, rewrite it **with** a hyphen.

- If it **has** a hyphen but **does not need** a hyphen, rewrite it **without** a hyphen.

- If it has a hyphen that is correct, write *correct*.

- If it is not hyphenated and does not need a hyphen, write *correct*.

Remember: Not all phrasal adjectives must have a hyphen to be correct.

1) (Correctly-hyphenated) phrasal adjectives can be easier for readers to understand.

   Correctly hyphenated

2) Phrasal adjectives that are (correctly hyphenated) can be easier to understand.

   correct

3) We asked if we could delete the (little used) program from our computers.

   little-used

4) Nana knitted me a (light blue) sweater that was (extremely thick) and warm.

   light-blue, correct (extremely thick)

5) The shards of broken glass were (razor-sharp.)

   razor sharp

6) The (individually wrapped) slices of cheese slowed me down as I made sandwiches for the whole team.

   correct

7) When I hurt my back, I spent a lot of time on the couch with a (hot water) bottle.

   hot-water

8) Do you think the glass is (half-empty) or (half-full)?

   half empty, half full

9) After 108 years, the (World Series-bound) were hoping to finally celebrate!

   correct

10) My cat Pixie is a (six-year old) tuxedo cat.

    six-year-old

Possessives: Assessment

Directions

Write the words according to the following directions.

Each correct answer is worth one point, for a total of 30 points.

Word	Possessive	Plural	Plural Possessive
tooth	*tooth's*	*teeth*	*teeth's*
box	*box's*	*boxes*	*boxes'*
nurse	*nurse's*	*nurses*	*nurses'*
Jones	*Jones's*	*Joneses*	*Joneses'*
kiss	*kiss's*	*kisses*	*kisses'*
witch	*witch's*	*witches*	*witches'*
country	*country's*	*countries*	*countries'*
puppy	*puppy's*	*puppies*	*puppies'*
man	*man's*	*men*	*men's*
woman	*woman's*	*women*	*women's*

30

Directions

Place apostrophes where they are needed in the following sentences.

Each correctly placed apostrophe is worth one point.

___ **1)** Deirdre couldn't wait to see her parents' reaction.
1

___ **2)** Our school band's original song was quite good.
1

___ **3)** All the horses' stalls need to be cleaned out.
1

___ **4)** Are all pigs' tails curly?
1

___ **5)** My mom's new job begins today.
1

___ **6)** Are you going over to Roberta White's house?
1

___ **7)** The three new students' work was best.
1

___ **8)** The two guests' gifts were funny.
1

___ **9)** We have to make fifteen other dancers' costumes.
1

___ **10)** My dog's left paw is injured.
1

___ **11)** Give me four dollars' worth of quarters, please.
1

___ **12)** Those countries' main exports are oil and coal.
1

___ **13)** Tony's speech was the best in the class.
1

___ **14)** The ladies' room is locked.
1

___ **15)** The women's room is locked.
1

___
15

Directions

Rewrite the following sentences using possessive adjectives.

Each correct answer is worth one point.

___ **16)** Hank did the laundry of the whole family last week.

  1   *Hank did the whole family's laundry last week.*

___ **17)** The hands of the pianist were long and slender.

  1   *The pianist's hands were long and slender.*

___ **18)** Glenn likes the symphonies of Beethoven.

  1   *Glenn likes Beethoven's symphonies.*

___ **19)** You should change the water of the goldfish.

  1   *You should change the goldfish's water.*

___ **20)** Bob isn't getting his usual vacation of three weeks this year.

  1   *Bob isn't getting his usual three weeks' vacation this year.*

___ **21)** The dishes of the cats are empty.

  1   *The cats' dishes are empty.*

___ **22)** Tonight we're going to a party at the house of the Joneses.

  1   *Tonight we're going to a party at the Joneses' house.*

___ **23)** The house of Ross is on the next street.

  1   *Ross's house is on the next street.*

___ **24)** Someone has borrowed the skates of Lee.

  1   *Someone has borrowed Lee's skates.*

___ **25)** The lounge of the teachers is located near the office.

  1   *The teachers' lounge is located near the office.*

___ **26)** The sails of all three boats need to be fixed.

  1   *All three boats' sails need to be fixed.*

___ **27)** Where is the room of the men?

  1   *Where is the men's room?*

___ **28)** The mother of Curtis is late.

  1   *Curtis's mother is late.*

___ **29)** Christians pray in the name of Jesus.

  1   *Christians pray in Jesus's name.*

___ **30)** There are two kids in the office of the nurse right now.

  1   *There are two kids in the nurse's office right now.*

15

Directions

Use each of the words below to create a possessive phrase. Then write an original sentence using the possessive phrase. Be sure you are using the noun as a possessive, not as a plural.

Answers will vary, but the possessive adjectives must be as shown. Give one point for correctly forming the possessive, and one for correctly using the possessive in a sentence.

Hercules	*Hercules's*
boy (singular)	*boy's*
boy (plural)	*boys'*
lady (singular)	*lady's*
lady (plural)	*ladies'*
Mr. Ellis	*Mr. Ellis's*
Chris	*Chris's*
week (singular)	*week's*
week (plural)	*weeks'*
Sheila	*Sheila's*

20

Total Points $\dfrac{64}{80} = 80\%$

80

Capitalization

Lesson 12: Capitalization

You already know some of the rules of capitalization, since they have been touched on in other lessons. This lesson compiles all of the rules in one place. The key phrase to remember is **proper names**. The proper names of almost everything, animate or inanimate, are capitalized.

A) Capitalize the names of persons.

Examples:

Sandra Wilson	MacDonald (both the M and the D are capitalized)
Mr. Charles F. Skinner	O'Brien (both the O and the B are capitalized)
Oz the Great and Powerful	John McCaffrey Jr. (abbreviations and letters after names are capitalized)

B) Capitalize geographical names.

Examples:

towns, cities	Anchorage, Kansas City, Rancho Cucamonga
counties	Harrison County
states	New Hampshire, Alaska, New South Wales
regions	the East, the Midwest, the Pacific Northwest

Note: The words *north*, *west*, *southeast*, and other directional words are not capitalized when they indicate direction, such as, *the south side of town* or *travel northwest for ten miles*. Capitalize them if they are referring to a certain section of a country or area, or if they are part of the proper name, such as North Carolina.

Examples:

countries	the United States of America, Colombia, Madagascar
continents	Australia, South America
islands	Prince Edward Island, the Hawaiian Islands
mountains	Mount Katahdin, Denali, the Alps
bodies of water	the Indian Ocean, Lake Wallenpaupack, the Colorado River
roads, highways	Route 10, New Seward Highway, Elm Street, Twenty-First Street
parks	Yellowstone National Park, Assateague Island National Seashore

Note: Words like *park*, *city*, *street*, and so on, are capitalized if they are part of a name. If they're not part of a name, they are lowercase like other common nouns.

C) Capitalize proper adjectives (adjectives made from proper nouns).

Examples: Greek theater, English literature, Italian shoes

D) Capitalize names of organizations, businesses, institutions, and governmental bodies.

Examples:	organizations	American Red Cross, Humane Society of Atlantic County
	businesses	Nordstrom, Western Airlines, Amazon, Samsung
	institutions	Columbia University, Service High School, St. Luke's Hospital
	government bodies	Congress, Federal Bureau of Investigation, Anderson City Council

Note: Don't capitalize words like *hotel*, *theater*, or *high school* unless they are part of a name.

E) Capitalize the names of historical events and periods, special events, and calendar items.

Examples:	historical events	Boston Tea Party, the Renaissance, World War I
	special events	March Madness, the Tour de France, Homecoming
	calendar items	Sunday, May, Halloween, Independence Day

Note: Don't capitalize the names of seasons (*summer*, *winter*, etc.) unless they are part of the name of an event (*Winter Carnival*, *Midsummer Classic*).

F) Capitalize the names of nationalities, races, and religions.

Examples:	nationalities	Canadians, European, Easter Islander
	races and ethnicities	Hispanic, Black, Caucasian, Pacific Islander
	religions	Muslim, Episcopalian, Eastern Orthodox

G) Capitalize the brand names of business products.

Examples: Math-U-See®, Demme Learning®, Spelling You See®

Note: Don't capitalize a noun following a brand name (Math-U-See® blocks, Demme Learning® curricula, Spelling You See® pencils).

H) **Capitalize the names of ships, planets, monuments, awards, and any other specific place, things, or event.**

Examples:	ships, trains	the Mayflower, the Orient Express aircraft, the Enola Gay, the Titan
	planets, stars	the North Star, Jupiter, the Milky Way

Note: *Sun* and *moon* are only capitalized when they are listed with the other bodies in our solar system. Earth is capitalized when it is a name (*I will return to Earth*) but not when it's preceded by an article (*I will return to the earth*).

Examples:	monuments, etc.	Washington Monument, Vietnam Veterans Memorial
	buildings	the Eiffel Tower, the Taj Mahal, the White House
	awards	the Oscar, Congressional Medal of Honor

I) **Capitalize school subjects only when they are languages or when naming a particular course. Otherwise, do not capitalize them.**

Example: Presently, I am taking English, science, Geometry I, Spanish, and economics.

J) **Capitalize titles and honorifics.**

1) **Capitalize the title of a person when it is used with their name.**

Examples: President Bush (but *the forty-third president*)

Mrs. Morrison

Dr. Jekyll (but *the mad doctor*)

Mr. Hyde

Lady Floribunda (but *my lady*)

Note: When a title is used alone in direct address, it is usually capitalized.

Examples: Excuse me, Doctor, your next patient is here.

It is very nice to meet you, General.

Be honest, Coach; what are our chances?

2) **Capitalize words showing family relationship used with or as a person's name but not preceded by an adjective.**

Examples: Aunt Mabel, Cousin It, Mom

my aunt, your cousin, Frank's mom

K) **Capitalize the first word and all other words in titles of books, periodicals, etc.,**
except articles, prepositions, and conjunctions (these words must be capitalized if they are the
first word of the title, however).

Examples: *Of Mice and Men*

"The Adventure of the Speckled Band"

"Jingle Bells"

Pride and Prejudice

James and the Giant Peach

L) **Capitalize words referring to the deity of a monotheistic religion.**
Don't capitalize *god* or other words referring to the deities of polytheistic religions and
belief systems.

Note: This rule is changing over time. Regardless of one's belief, the name of the deity (*God*,
Allah) should be capitalized like any other proper name. Pronouns referring to the deity may be
capitalized or not, according to preference. Regardless of which is chosen, be consistent.

Examples: God and His universe (or *God and his universe*)

The people came to Jesus and they worshipped Him. (or *The people came to Jesus and
they worshipped him.*)

The god of Islam is Allah.

The god of Christianity is God.

The Aztec god in the form of a feathered serpent was Quetzalcoatl. (Note that *god* is
lowercase. This is because the Aztecs had many gods; they were polytheistic.)

The proofreading symbol that means "capitalize this letter" is a triple underline, like this:

Example: bob thompson

Capitalization: Exercise A

Directions

Circle the letter of the correct sentence. Use the lesson notes to determine which is correct and why.

1) **(A)** His store is on Front Street in Burlington.
   B) His store is on front street in Burlington.

2) **A)** We crossed the Snake river.
   (B) We crossed the Snake River.

3) **A)** He now lives in california.
   (B) He now lives in California.

4) **(A)** Did you fly over South America?
   B) Did you fly over south America?

5) **(A)** He took a picture of Pikes Peak.
   B) He took a picture of Pikes peak.

6) **(A)** City streets in the West are often wide.
   B) City streets in the west are often wide.

7) **(A)** Yellowstone National Park has many geysers.
   B) Yellowstone national park has many geysers.

8) **(A)** The city of Columbus is the capital of Ohio.
   B) The City of Columbus is the capital of Ohio.

9) **A)** The hurricane swept over the gulf of Mexico.
   (B) The hurricane swept over the Gulf of Mexico.

10) **(A)** Drive east on U.S. Highway 35.
    B) Drive East on U.S. Highway 35.

11) **A)** We are proud of our State parks.
    (B) We are proud of our state parks.

12) **(A)** I live on Forty-Fifth Street.
    B) I live on Forty-fifth street.

13) **(A)** The headquarters is in Travis County.
    B) The headquarters is in Travis county.

14) **A)** The Vikings called the atlantic ocean the sea of darkness.

     B) The Vikings called the Atlantic Ocean the Sea of Darkness.

15) **A)** The states of the Midwest are referred to as the nation's breadbasket.

     B) The states of the midwest are referred to as the nation's breadbasket.

16) **A)** A three-lane highway can be dangerous.

     B) A three-lane Highway can be dangerous.

17) **A)** I have a map of the Virgin Islands.

     B) I have a map of the Virgin islands.

18) **A)** New York city is the largest city on the east coast.

     B) New York City is the largest city on the East Coast.

19) **A)** The Great Salt Lake is near the Nevada border.

     B) The Great Salt lake is near the Nevada Border.

20) **A)** His address is 2009 Bell Avenue.

     B) His address is 2009 Bell avenue.

Capitalization: Exercise B

Directions

Draw a triple line under all of the letters that should be capitalized in the following sentences.

1) mr. ronson mentioned the fact that mercury and venus are closer to earth than jupiter.

2) every freshman at jefferson high school knows that they will take at least three years of english and two years of math.

3) while in the city of washington, we saw ford's theatre, where lincoln was shot.

4) a methodist, a muslim, and a roman catholic conducted an interesting panel discussion.

5) since I plan to study medicine at northwestern university, I'm taking latin and biology 1.

6) after I had gone to the grocery store at the corner of thirtieth street and stonewall avenue, I stopped at the twin oaks lumber company, which is two blocks south of cooper avenue.

7) vacationing in the west, we saw electric peak, which is on the northern boundary of yellowstone national park; we also saw the devil's tower, which is in northeastern wyoming.

8) we drove along ohio drive and saw the lincoln memorial, which is the site of dr. martin luther king jr.'s famous "I have a dream" speech.

9) in the spring, usually the first saturday after easter, the women's missionary society, a baptist organization, gives a picnic for our class.

10) leaving ecuador in south america on a banana boat named *bonanza*, they went through the panama canal and sailed through the caribbean sea to nassau in the bahamas.

Capitalization: Exercise C

Directions

Draw a triple line under all of the letters that should be capitalized in the following sentences.

1) speaking to the seniors of westfield high school, mr. carter praised *the tragedy of american compassion*, a book by marvin olasky.

2) on the sunday before labor day, we drove as far as the murphy motel, a mile west of salem, virginia; the manager, mr. kelly, proudly announced that he was a member of the virginia tourist court association.

3) waiting for a city bus at the corner of twenty-first street and hampton drive, we admired the anne klein clothing in dillard's window display.

4) dad and his brother, my uncle julian, told me about rockefeller center and about the shops on fifth avenue in new york city.

5) professor massey studied at the library of congress and the folger shakespeare library during july and august.

6) althea gibson's autobiography *I always wanted to* be somebody* was published by harper & row.

   *****Note:*** *To is capitalized. If your student doesn't capitalize it, tell them that it should be capitalized and ask them if they can figure out why. In this sentence,* to *is not a preposition, but a part of the infinitive* to be. *Since it's a verbal and not a preposition, both* to *and* be *should be capitalized.*

7) I especially like the photograph, made by alaska airlines, of denali in alaska.

8) in his junior year at sheridan high school, uncle rufus studied latin, french, english, geometry, and art.

9) professor walker told us that the gods of the ancient greeks did not stay on mount olympus all the time but chose to mingle with humans on earth.

10) after the texans fought so bravely against the forces of general santa anna in 1836, the alamo became famous as a memorial to texas liberty, a symbol of american freedom like the statue of liberty.

Application & Enrichment

The Subjunctive Mood

We know that verbs have *tenses*, but did you know that they also have *moods*? A verb's mood can be applied to any one of the verb tenses we have learned. The good news is that you already know two of the three main moods in English!

Indicative mood: the verb form used to make statements and questions

This is the form of the verb we use almost all the time, and it's the one that we studied in our previous verb tense activities.

> **Examples:**   The dog *raced* to the end of the driveway to meet me.
>
> ***Will*** you *be attending* the Governor's Ball?
>
> I *have* a drama club meeting right after school.

Imperative mood: the verb form used to give commands

The imperative mood is used for commands. It has the *understood* ***you*** as a subject.

> **Examples:**   *Make* your bed and *fold* your laundry, please.

Subjunctive mood: the verb form used to talk about things that are wished for but that are not true

This is the mood you might not be familiar with yet. The subjunctive is used to talk about situations that didn't happen but could have, or things that might happen. It's also used to describe possible consequences, wishes, suggestions, contrary-to-fact scenarios, and other imaginary or potential situations.

If I *were* taller, I would play volleyball. (*If I were taller, but I'm not.*)

The professor suggested that Jenn *prepare* her presentation carefully. (*The professor is giving Jenn a suggestion.*)

We request that he *return* the overdue library book as soon as possible. (*He hasn't returned the overdue book yet, but we wish he would.*)

Here are a few important things to notice about the subjunctive:

- It is usually found in a subordinate (dependent) clause. In the examples above, the subjunctive verb is in clauses beginning with *if* or ***that***. The dependent clauses all show things that either haven't happened yet or that are impossible.

- The subject takes a different form of the verb than we would expect. Normally, we would see *I was, Jenn prepares,* and *he returns*; not *I were, Jenn prepare,* or *he return*. The subjunctive of most verbs is formed by dropping the *-s* from the third person singular form of the verb—the form used with *he, she,* and *it*. ***To be*** and ***to have*** are a little different:

indicative mood	subjunctive mood
am, are, is	be
was, were	be
has, have	have

There are certain words that are hints about when you might want to use the subjunctive mood. We've already identified ***if*** and ***that*** as words frequently used with this mood. There are several verbs that, when used in the independent clause, can signal the subjunctive as well: ***ask, demand, order, insist, suggest,*** and ***wish*** are some of them.

Like many of the topics we've discussed, properly using the subjunctive can make your writing appear more polished and professional. This is especially beneficial in formal writing situations, such as work or school. You may rarely hear it today, but if you wish to use proper grammar, learn to recognize when the subjunctive should be used for your formal writing—and then use it!

Directions

Rewrite the following sentences to be in the subjunctive mood.

1) The lawyer demanded that his client is set free.

> *The lawyer demanded that his client be set free.*

2) If I was to give you the money, could you get me a ticket, too

> *If I were to give you the money, could you get me a ticket, too?*

3) Juan wished that he was on vacation somewhere sunny.

> *Juan wished that he were on vacation somewhere sunny.*

4) All I ask is that I am allowed to knit quietly, in peace.

> *All I ask is that I be allowed to knit quietly, in peace.*

5) If the football team was to play defense, they would win more games.

> *If the football team were to play defense, they would win more games.*

Capitalization: Assessment

Directions

Some of the following sentences are correct, but some need capitalization. If the sentence is correct, write **correct** beneath it. If capitalization is needed, draw a triple underline beneath the letters that should be capitalized.

Each correctly corrected capitalization counts for one point. If capitalization is not needed, the sentence is worth one point."

___ **1)** In the fall, everyone looks forward to the football season.

1   *correct*

___ **2)** Football fans can see their favorite high school and college teams play on saturday and their

2   favorite professional teams on sunday.

___ **3)** Last weekend, I saw indiana play penn state.

3

___ **4)** Kay's aunt introduced her to the captain of the *queen elizabeth II.*

2

___ **5)** The greeks believed that their deities met on mount olympus to listen to zeus, the king of

4   the gods.

___ **6)** Ann likes geography and history, but she does the best in english and french.

2

___ **7)** Chief justice roberts explained the ruling of the supreme court.

4

___ **8)** On July 4, the Bayshore Mall puts on a spectacular fireworks display.

1   *correct*

___ **9)** The *titanic* sank after hitting an iceberg off the coast of newfoundland.

2

___**10)** My aunt went to amsterdam to see rembrandt's *the night watch.*

5

26

___**11)** Mail the letter to the union of south africa and the package to genoa, italy.
5

___**12)** This year, palm sunday is the last sunday in march.
4

___**13)** Among the early settlers were roman catholics and congregationalists.
3

___**14)** like other native north american tribes, the ancient iroquois believed in many gods.
4

___**15)** The department of agriculture publishes many pamphlets that are useful for home gardeners.
2

___**16)** Did aunt josie send you that straw hat from costa rica?
4

___**17)** The *windy jane* is a small, white sailboat.
2

___**18)** Last winter, Carrie had an ice boat on greenwood lake.
2

___**19)** In history and also in spanish, we are studying the european renaissance.
3

___**20)** One woman is armenian; the other is greek.
2

___
31

___**21)** nan and I are spending the summer at camp medomak in washington, maine.
5

___**22)** Tommy has a new English bicycle, a gift from his aunt.
1   *correct*

___**23)** Suddenly I saw the boeing 747 darting across the sky.
1

___**24)** Here is a new series of Norwegian airmail stamps.

1   *correct*

___**25)** The waters of the Mediterranean are very blue.

1   *correct*

___**26)** The table is made of asian teakwood.

1

___**27)** The Acme Tractor Company is looking for a qualified computer analyst.

1   *correct*

___**28)** Have you ever seen a Mexican jumping bean?

1   *correct*

___**29)** We heard the performance of Verdi's *aida*.

1

___**30)** My sister is taking english, math II, social studies, biology, and french.

3

16

___**31)** Just then, I noticed her new persian rug.

1

___**32)** Is the goldstar bus company still on strike?

3

___**33)** Silk is an important Japanese export.

1   *correct*

___**34)** Jerry lives on the west side of oak street.

2

___**35)** Sometimes, the boys go fishing on Lake Oswego.

1   *correct*

___**36)** In Aspen, Colorado, I learned to ride a horse.

1   *correct*

___**37)** She is traveling on northwest airlines.

2

___**38)** My favorite show is sponsored by cocoa krispies cereal.

2

___**39)** Colgate has introduced a new kind of toothpaste.

1   *correct*

___**40)** Octopuses lurk in the mediterranean sea.

2

$$\overline{\overline{}}$$
16

$$\overline{\overline{}} \textit{Total Points} \quad \frac{71}{89} = 80\%$$
89

Punctuation/Capitalization Review

Lesson 13: Punctuation/Capitalization Review
Exercise A

Directions

Using everything you have learned about punctuation and capitalization, punctuate the following sentences correctly. Draw a triple underline beneath any letters that should be capitalized.

1) Our national heroes, people like <u>A</u>braham <u>L</u>incoln, <u>M</u>artin <u>L</u>uther <u>K</u>ing <u>J</u>r., and <u>C</u>esar <u>C</u>havez, fought for these rights: life, liberty, and equality.

2) Rod <u>E</u>vans, sailing over the last hurdle, won the race easily; roger <u>E</u>vans, his brother, came in a distant second.

3) "I knew you'd make it, <u>R</u>od!" shouted <u>W</u>inston. "when are you headed to the <u>O</u>lympics? your father said last night, 'my son rod is going to be an all-american this year!'"

4) Rosemary is knitting her first sweater, a soft, cuddly wool one with no sleeves. She is making it according to the directions in the <u>M</u>ay issue of <u>S</u>eventeen magazine.

5) John does, I believe, still live at 268 <u>F</u>airway <u>L</u>ane, <u>F</u>airbanks, <u>A</u>laska.

6) Father's <u>D</u>ay comes on the third <u>S</u>unday in <u>J</u>une; mother's <u>D</u>ay is on the second <u>S</u>unday in <u>M</u>ay.

7) Sofia dreams of doing research at the <u>R</u>ockefeller <u>N</u>ational <u>L</u>aboratory in <u>A</u>lbany, <u>N</u>ew <u>Y</u>ork.

8) I've carefully studied lesson 24, "punctuating quotations," in our textbook <u>A</u>dventures in <u>P</u>unctuation; therefore, I feel prepared for the test tomorrow.

9) Wisteria, a lovely purple flower, was named for <u>C</u>aspar <u>W</u>istar, an 18th century anatomist, and jimson weed was named after <u>J</u>amestown, <u>V</u>irginia.

10) A computer can be used for making lists of things to do, keeping track of household accounts, and doing your homework; and term papers done on a computer always look nicer.

Punctuation/Capitalization Review: Exercise B

Directions

Using everything you have learned about punctuation and capitalization, punctuate the following sentences correctly. Draw a triple underline beneath any letters that should be capitalized.

1) The race was over; the jockey leapt from her horse and smilingly accepted the glittering, shimmering gold cup.

2) Mr. Cameron, our shop teacher, announced, "Bring the following supplies: wood, nails, and glue."

3) "The girls' mittens are missing," said Mom. "They said they left them in the pockets of their Wilson High School jackets."

4) "Have you seen Kevin Costner's movie Dances with Wolves?" Cara asked.

5) Casey's story "The Night They Burned the Outhouse" will appear in this month's issue of Sanitation Gazette.

6) "I think I should point out," said Mr. Henries, the store manager, "that Michael's dog isn't welcome here."

7) "Watch out for practical jokers!" yelled Mike. "It's Halloween, you know!"

8) "Did Mrs. Finley say, 'In my opinion, Die Hard is a Christmas movie,'" asked John, "or am I hearing things?"

9) "First I read the sports section of today's Washington Post," said Jim, "and then I did the crossword puzzle."

10) The judge, staring with a ferocious scowl at the sneering, defiant prisoner, asked, "Do you plead guilty or not guilty?"

Punctuation/Capitalization Review: Exercise C

Directions

Using everything you have learned about punctuation and capitalization, punctuate the following sentences correctly. Underline any letters that should be capitalized three times. Remember: titles that are also appositives are not set apart by commas because they are already set apart by italics, underlining, or punctuation marks.

1) "can you lend me five dollars for a week or so, old buddy?" asked mr. gardner, dad's best friend.

2) "Jim, the cleaning woman is here, but she said she doesn't do windows!" yelled mom.

3) His program, which we watch regularly, is on sunday afternoons.

4) "People who live in glass houses shouldn't throw stones," said ms. phillips.

5) "why, even I can work this gadget, mary!" exclaimed elaine.

6) "it was jean, as a matter of fact, who memorized the poem 'stopping by woods on a snowy evening' from our poetry anthology america's major poets," said robert.

7) The test was long and difficult; however, everyone finished.

8) His grades are as follows: english, his favorite class, an A; history, a really tough class, a B; science, his least favorite, a C; and math, a B.

9) The sermon opened with a reading of deuteronomy 3:24 from the king james version of the bible.

10) "how," richard asked, mopping his brow listlessly, "do people survive in this climate?"

Application & Enrichment
Paraphrasing

Directions

This is a poem written by a young girl introduced in an earlier lesson. Riva Minska was a prisoner in the German concentration camp Mittelsteine during World War II. Parse and diagram lines 1 and 13. Then paraphrase the entire poem.

"Why?"
Written by Riva Minska, Number 55082
Camp Mittelsteine, Germany
January 14, 1945

Translated from the Yiddish
by Ruth Minsky Sender, Free Person
New York City, U.S.A.
1980

adv adv pro av pp art   n

1) All alone, I stare (at the window)

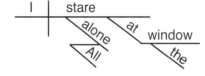

2) Feeling my soul in me cry,

3) Hearing the painful screams of my heart

4) Calling silently: Why?

5) Why are your dreams scattered, destroyed?

6) Why are you put in this cage?

7) Why is the world silently watching?

8) Why can't they hear your rage?

9) Why is the barbed wire holding me prisoner,

10) Block to freedom my way?

11) Why do I still keep waiting and dreaming

12) Hoping...maybe...someday...

pro av   pp   pro art   adj   n

13) I see (above me) the snow-covered mountains,

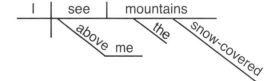

14) Majestic, proud, and high.

15) If like a free bird I could reach their peaks

16) Maybe (from there) the world will hear my cry...

17) Why?

Punctuation/Capitalization Review: Assessment

Remember to use the lesson notes if you need help with any part of this review.

Directions

Add the necessary punctuation and capitalization to the following sentences.

Each correct punctuation is worth one point.

_____ **1)** "the teacher said, 'I will assign no homework tonight'!" she yelled jubilantly.
   6

_____ **2)** "over the drinking fountain at school," bob reported, "there is a sign that says,
   13   'old faceful.'"

_____ **3)** as the president of the united states entered, the band played "hail to the chief."
   8

_____ **4)** john adams and thomas jefferson, old rivals, died on the same day, the fourth of july.
   9

_____ **5)** most of the engineers were pleased with the new design, but helen had doubts about it.
   3

_____ **6)** to eat, the little old man from china used chopsticks.
   3

_____ **7)** mrs. curtis's shoes hurt her feet, but she wore them anyway.
   4

_____ **8)** "the parents are invited to the teachers' meeting," said mrs. haynes.
   7

_____ **9)** the new high school has many excellent features; however, it needs more equipment
   3   in the gym.

_____ **10)** this traffic control will be introduced in the following cities: buffalo, new york;
   20   st. louis, missouri; dallas, texas; and los angeles, california.

_____ **11)** "we'll soon catch this culprit; he has left several fingerprints on this glass," said
   7   detective grogan.

_____ **12)** the following were thomas's ambitions: to go to harvard, to graduate summa cum
   10   laude, and to get a job in a prestigious new york law firm.

_____ **13)** "I did not read this week's newsweek," said frank, "but I heard there was an article
   15   called 'life on other planets.'"

_____ **14)** "the waitresses' names appear on their checks," said the manager. "please let me
   9   know if there is any problem."

___ **15)** we were so thirsty after our run; milk or water or even ink would have been refreshing!
  2

___ **16)** the happy, tired, victorious crew staggered over the rocks and fell onto the sand.
  3

___ **17)** roy shouted in anger, "you heard my dad say, 'I won't allow you boys to go out tonight'!"
  8

___ **18)** "we can now hope," said dr. peters, chief of surgery at harbor general hospital, "for a
  15 complete recovery."

___ **19)** the call of the wild, jack london's great novel, is popular with alaskans.
  10

___ **20)** "the lucky person who enjoys reading is never lonely," said my english teacher.
  5

  160

Directions

Punctuate the following **possessive phrases** correctly.

Each correctly punctuated sentence is worth one point.

___ **21)** The three contestants' entries were all good.
  1

___ **22)** The judges' work could be observed by visiting their courtrooms.
  1

___ **23)** One judge's choice was different from the rest.
  1

___ **24)** That is one of this year's best new television series.
  1

___ **25)** The story's ending leaves many readers puzzled.
  1

___ **26)** The four ships' cargoes are on the pier.
  1

___ **27)** The drill team girls' jackets are at the cleaners.
  1

___ **28)** Three women's cars were left in the parking lot.
  1

___ **29)** The customer's* complaints did not impress the manager.
  1

___ **30)** Have you read the exciting tales of Ulysses's adventures?
  1

  * Either customer's or customers' is correct.

  10

Directions

Put colons where they are needed in the following sentences.

Each correctly placed colon is worth one point.

____ **31)** The book has photographs of some of the most beautiful mountain ranges in the
1   world: the Himalayas, the Andes, the Alps, and the Rockies.

____ **32)** Here is a list of the possible times for our meeting: 12:30, 2:00, or 5:00.
4

____ **33)** I arrived at the station at 3:30 in the morning.
1

____ **34)** You will need to find the following: a fishing rod, some night crawlers, a few
1   hooks, and a bag to take home any fish we catch.

____ **35)** If I wake up after 7:30, I can't get to school before 9:00.
2

____ **36)** Whenever I see a poster of Italy, I think of all the wonderful things I ate there:
1   delicious cream sauces, ripe black olives, succulent meats, and golden cheeses.

____ **37)** The train will depart from Anchorage at 7:15 and arrive in Fairbanks at 4:30.
2

____ **38)** Please give this message to the following people: Sandy Pressman, Judy Pruitt,
1   Mike Scott, and Alex Wolfson.

____ **39)** If you want to be in Fresno before 4:00, you should leave here by 10:30.
2

____ **40)** Tell me which of these presents you would prefer: a bicycle, a canoe, a radio, or a dog.
1

16

Directions

Insert semicolons where they are needed in the following sentences. Correct existing punctuation, if necessary.

Each correct punctuation is worth one point.

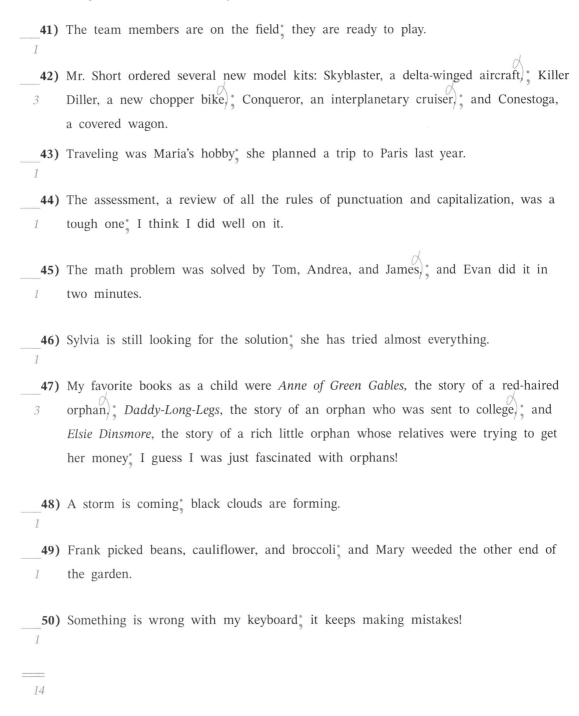

___ **41)** The team members are on the field; they are ready to play.

1

___ **42)** Mr. Short ordered several new model kits: Skyblaster, a delta-winged aircraft; Killer
3   Diller, a new chopper bike; Conqueror, an interplanetary cruiser; and Conestoga,
a covered wagon.

___ **43)** Traveling was Maria's hobby; she planned a trip to Paris last year.

1

___ **44)** The assessment, a review of all the rules of punctuation and capitalization, was a
1   tough one; I think I did well on it.

___ **45)** The math problem was solved by Tom, Andrea, and James; and Evan did it in
1   two minutes.

___ **46)** Sylvia is still looking for the solution; she has tried almost everything.

1

___ **47)** My favorite books as a child were *Anne of Green Gables,* the story of a red-haired
3   orphan; *Daddy-Long-Legs,* the story of an orphan who was sent to college; and
Elsie Dinsmore, the story of a rich little orphan whose relatives were trying to get
her money; I guess I was just fascinated with orphans!

___ **48)** A storm is coming; black clouds are forming.

1

___ **49)** Frank picked beans, cauliflower, and broccoli; and Mary weeded the other end of
1   the garden.

___ **50)** Something is wrong with my keyboard; it keeps making mistakes!

1

14

Directions

Insert commas where they are needed.

Each correctly placed comma is worth one point.

    51) We first heard this story in Sydney, Australia, during our vacation.
   2

    52) On December 31, 1977, a stranger arrived in Nestor, North Dakota.
   3

    53) Between January 31, 1978, and February 23, 1978, he worked in the garage of his house.
   4

    54) On November 22, 1978, the stranger went to Grand Rapids, Michigan.
   3

    55) He returned on December 1, 1978, with a large box.
   2

    56) On December 10, 1978, young Tim Hartley peeked into the garage.
   2

    57) From that day until the Hartleys moved to Kingsport, Tennessee, Tim told wild
   2   tales of what he had seen in that garage.

    58) Between February 24, 1979, and March 15, 1979, neighbors heard strange noises
   4   coming from the garage.

    59) The neighbors met on March 16, 1979, and decided to complain to the police.
   2

    60) The police visited the house on March 16, 1979, and again on March 17, 1979, but
   4   no one seemed to be at home.

    61) The police obtained a search warrant on March 18, 1979.
   1

    62) Half of the people of Nestor, North Dakota, were watching as the police entered
   2   the garage.

    63) All they found was an empty box and a newspaper dated February 28, 2089.
   1

   32

Directions

In each sentence below, there is a comma split. All of the commas in each sentence and the lines below them are numbered. Identify the comma split and write its number in the space next to the sentence number. On the numbered lines below, write what the comma is splitting on the appropriate line. For the correctly placed commas, write the comma rule "buzzword" on the numbered line.

Correctly identifying the number of the comma split is worth two points; the numbered lines below the sentences are worth one point each.

___*2*___ **64)** In the business world of the future, machines designed for specific functions, will do a
2   1   2

be completely replaced.
lot of the work which we now do ourselves, but I don't believe the human mind can ever
                                                                3

be completely replaced.

___ **#1**   *introductory element*   _____
1

___ **#2**   *splits subject* (machines) *and verb* (will do)   _____
1

___ **#3**   *compound sentence*   _____
1

___*5*___ **65)** Yes, we have machines which can do math functions, keep track of data, and check our
2   1   2   3

spelling, but only a human being can perform, certain types of work.
            4   5

___ **#1**   *introductory element*   _____
1

___ **#2**   *items in a series*   _____
1

___ **#3**   *items in a series*   _____
1

___ **#4**   *compound sentence*   _____
1

___ **#5**   *splits verb* (perform) *and direct object* (types)   _____
1

___5___ **66)** If we wish to communicate ideas to other people, we often use jokes, examples, and
 2   1   2   3

analogies as a means of explaining complex, detailed, concepts.
                                                                        4   5

___ **#1** *introductory element* _____
 1

___ **#2** *items in a series* _____
 1

___ **#3** *items in a series* _____
 1

___ **#4** *two adjectives tests* _____
 1

___ **#5** *splits modifier* (detailed) *and its noun* (concepts) _____
 1

___1___ **67)** Even a machine which has been programmed to write, could not come up with jokes or
 2   1

plays on words, those little extras that even an average, well-educated person would use.
                          2   3

___ **#1** *splits subject* (machine) *and verb* (could come) _____
 1

___ **#2** *appositive phrases* _____
 1

___ **#3** *two adjectives tests* _____
 1

___*1*___ **68)** Whenever our future employment is looking more and more, doubtful because machines
2   1

are taking over, remember that an educated human being, using all his or her creative
                     2   3

talents to the utmost, can never be completely replaced by a machine.
                     4

___ **#1** *splits linking verb* (looking) *and predicate adjective* (doubtful)
1

___ **#2** *introductory element*
1

___ **#3** *nonessentinal modifier*
1

___ **#4** *nonessentinal modifier*
1

═══
30

Directions

Rewrite the following dialogue, using correct paragraphing, capitalization, and punctuation.

69) Sean and Jason walked slowly into Mrs. Finley's classroom Sean sat down, put his books under
    his desk, and leaned over to Jason hey he said are you as worried about this test as I am are you
    kidding said Jason I worked until midnight you mean you studied asked Sean, beginning to chew
    his fingernails I kind of thought I'd try to fake it are you out of your mind Jason hissed I studied for
    two hours I looked over all of my notes and went over the review worksheets Sean smiled weakly at
    Jason wow he said looking over your notes and going over the review sheets what a great idea wish
    I'd thought of it Jason stared at Sean sadly it's a little late now, pal

Each correct paragraph break is worth one point.

___   *Sean and Jason walked slowly into Mrs. Finley's classroom. Sean sat down, put his books under*
11   *his desk, and leaned over to Jason.* *"Hey," he said, "are you as worried about this test as I am?"*

___   *"Are you kidding?" said Jason. "I worked until midnight." (or ...midnight!")*
9

___   *"You mean you studied?" asked Sean, beginning to chew his fingernails. "I kind of thought I'd*
9   *try to fake it."*

___   *"Are you out of your mind?" Jason hissed. "I studied for two hours. I looked over all of my notes*
11   *and went over the review worksheets."*

___
15

Sean smiled weakly at Jason. "Wow!" he said. "Looking over your notes and going over the review sheets! What a great idea! Wish I'd thought of it." (note that these sentences could end with either exclamation points or periods.)

___
6

Jason stared at Sean sadly. "It's a little late now, pal." or, Jason stared at Sean. "Sadly, it's a little late now, pal."

===
61

=== *Total Points* $\dfrac{258}{323} = 80\%$
323

Pronoun-Antecedent Agreement

Lesson 14: Pronoun-Antecedent Agreement

When we learned about pronouns in Level 3, we learned that an antecedent is the noun that the pronoun stands for. A pronoun must agree with its antecedent in **number**, **gender**, and **person**. (Lesson 15 is about subject-verb agreement. For now, just know that singular nouns and pronouns take singular verbs, and plural nouns and pronouns take plural verbs.)

Number refers to whether a pronoun is **singular or plural**. Think about what is being said in the sentence. The examples provide a rephrasing to help clarify why the pronoun is singular or plural.

1) The following pronouns are **singular**. They will take the singular form of the verb.

each	one	everybody	someone
either	anybody	everyone	nobody
neither	anyone	somebody	no one
she	her	hers	—
he	him	his	—
it	it	its	—

Examples: **Each** of the soldiers was ready for inspection. (*Each individual soldier was ready for inspection.*)

Notice that, although **soldiers** is plural, the pronoun is referring to the individual soldiers who make up the group of soldiers.

Everyone has a right to their own opinion. (*Each individual person has a right...*)

Someone leaves their books under the tree every day. (*A single person leaves their books.*)

2) The following pronouns can be **either singular or plural**, depending on the antecedent. The verb will also be either singular or plural to match.

all	any	some	none

Examples: **All** of the soldiers were ready for **their** inspection. (*The **soldiers** were ready as individuals making up a collective group.*)

Compare this to the first sentence in the examples given for number 1, above.

All of the pizza is gone because John ate **it**! (*The singular **pizza**, in **its** entirety, is gone.*)

3) Two or more singular antecedents joined by **or** or **nor** are treated as a singular.

Examples: Either Jack **or** Hal will bring **his** tape recorder. (*Because Jack and Hal are both boys, we use the masculine singular pronoun **his**.*)

Neither rain **nor** snow **is** enough to stop the mail service. (*Both **rain** and **snow** take the singular form of the verb. Because they are connected by the conjunction **nor**, they are treated as singular and require the singular verb **is**. Compare that to the following sentence that uses **and**.*)

Rain **and** snow **are** difficult to drive in because **they** can make the road slippery. (*The conjunction **and** adds two singular nouns together to create a plural noun. The verb **are** and the pronoun **they** are both plural because of that.*)

Gender refers to whether the pronoun is masculine, feminine, or gender neutral. In English, only singular pronouns have a gender.

Pronoun Form	Masculine	Feminine	Gender Neutral (or unknown)
subjective	he	she	it
objective	him	her	it
possessive*	his	her *or* hers	its
subjective	—	—	they
objective	—	—	them
possessive*	—	—	their *or* theirs

*Remember, possessive pronouns do not get apostrophes.

> The whale was spraying water from **its** spout. (gender neutral)

> The letter carrier said **he** was tired. (masculine)

> The waitress wrote our order in **her** notepad. (feminine)

> The best student wins a scholarship to the college of **their** choice. (gender unknown)

It is generally used for inanimate objects or animals, while *they* is increasingly used for people when their gender is unknown or unspecified.

A word about *they*:

They can be *either singular or plural,* but it **always** takes a plural verb.

They, their, and **theirs** are plural pronouns that take the place of a noun referring to more than one person.

> My grandparents **are** very proud of **their** pesto recipe. (***Grandparents** is a plural noun; it takes the plural verb **are** and the plural pronoun **their**.*)

In speech and informal writing, however, we also use **they, their,** and **theirs** as a singular pronoun when the gender of the noun being replaced is not known.

> **One** of the students left **their** jacket in the auditorium.

> **Each** of the attendees said that **they are** enjoying the presentation. (*Notice the plural verb **are** must be used with **they,** even though it is replacing the singular pronoun **each**.*)

As mentioned, using *they* as a singular, gender neutral pronoun is less formal, and some academic or professional readers may not approve. If you are writing a formal paper or letter, it is best to revise the sentence so you don't need a pronoun at all. It's not as difficult as it may sound!

> **One** of the students left **a** jacket in the auditorium.

> **Each** of the attendees is enjoying the presentation.

Person refers to the perspective of the writer or speaker:

Personal Pronouns	Perspective
I, me, my, mine **we, us, our, ours**	**First Person** The author or speaker is talking about themselves and their point of view. Stories written with this perspective make the reader feel as though the action is happening directly to them. Diaries and letters are examples of first-person writing.
you, your, yours	**Second Person** The author or speaker is **directly addressing** someone else. Instructions and directions are examples of writing in second-person perspective.
he, him, his **she, her, hers** **it, its** **they, them, their, theirs**	**Third Person** The author or speaker is talking **about** someone or something else. Stories written in this perspective tell the reader what someone or something is doing. News articles and reports are written in third person perspective.

Person should be consistent throughout the sentence.

> **Examples:** **One** should never let **your** disappointment show.

This sentence starts in third person and switches to second person.

> Better: **One** should never let **their** (or **one's**) disappointment show.
>
> *or*
>
> **You** should never let **your** disappointment show.

> **I** find that driving at night is hard on **your** eyes.

This sentence starts in first person and switches to second person.

> Better: **I** find that night driving is hard on **my** eyes.

Pronoun-Antecedent Agreement: Exercise A

Directions

Change the pronouns to correct any error in agreement with the antecedent.

1) Neither the buyer nor the seller had made up ~~its~~ *their* mind.

2) Everyone has a right to ~~your~~ *their* own opinion.

3) Each of the winning essays had ~~their~~ *its* good points.

       Their *is used with people, while* its *is used with inanimate objects.*

4) Will each student please turn in ~~my~~ *their* schedule tomorrow?

5) One should always call ahead for ~~your~~ *one's* or *their* hotel reservation.

       Also correct: You *should always call ahead for* your *hotel reservation.*

6) Each of us needs to start thinking about ~~their~~ *our* career now.

7) If one tries hard enough, ~~you~~ *one* or *they* can usually finish the reports in an hour.

       Also correct: If you *try hard enough,* you *can usually finish the reports in an hour.*

8) Everyone applying for the scholarship must bring ~~your~~ *their* birth certificate.

9) Susannah has not written ~~our~~ *her* thank-you notes.

10) Everybody in the office has made ~~his~~ *their* vacation plans.

       Unless we know that everyone in the office is male, we should use their.

Directions

In each blank, write a pronoun that will agree with its antecedent.

11) A person should not be too demanding of _____ friends.

     their

12) The mailman brought Jack and Ray the books _____ had ordered.

     they

13) Either Norma or Jill will stay after school so that _____ can help decorate.

     she

14) Several of the students refused to eat _____ food.

     their

15) Each of the seals caught the fish that were thrown to _____.

     it

Directions

Revise the following sentences so that they do not include pronouns.

Answers will vary; one possible solution is given.

16) It is important for students to plan their time for homework.

     It is important for students to plan a time for homework.

17) The utility room is where they kept cleaning supplies.

     The cleaning supplies were kept in the utility room.

18) Doug has worked at many different locations and he is quite personable.

     Doug, who is quite personable, has worked at many different locations.

Pronoun-Antecedent Agreement: Exercise B

Directions

Some of the following sentences contain errors in pronoun-antecedent agreement. If so, cross out the incorrect pronoun and write the correct form. If there are no errors, write **correct** below the sentence.

1) One of my aunts takes a great deal of pride in her furniture.

   correct

2) Knowing this, nobody in our family puts ~~his~~ *their* feet on chairs or bounces on the bed at her house.

3) One of her brothers used to think ~~they~~ *he* should be an exception to the rule.

4) Uncle Charlie would come home late at night, undress in the dark, and dive into bed, nearly
   knocking all of the slats out of ~~its~~ *their* places.

5) Each one of these plunges took ~~their~~ *its* toll on the rickety bed.

6) At first, both Aunt Mary and my mother offered their advice and asked him to be careful.

   correct

7) Any other person would have mended ~~his~~ *their* ways, but not Charlie!

8) Late one night, there was a loud crash, and everyone ran out of ~~its~~ *their* rooms to investigate.

9) No one could believe ~~one's~~ *their* eyes! Charlie was lying on the floor, groaning loudly, because Aunt

   Mary had moved the bed!

10) If anybody asks you why Charlie suddenly reformed, tell ~~him~~ *them* that one day, Aunt Mary merely

    decided to rearrange her furniture.

Directions

In each blank, write a pronoun that will agree with the antecedent.

11) Both of the boys forgot _____ books.

      their

12) Everyone needs _____ own pen.

      their

13) Neither man apologized for _____ mistake.

      his

14) Each of the players felt that _____ had failed the coach.

      they

15) When Susan sees one of her girlfriends, she always talks to _____.

      her

Directions

Revise the following sentences so that they do not include pronouns.

Answers will vary; one possible solution is given.

16) A person who masters communication can succeed in any of their chosen fields.

      A person who masters communication can succeed in any chosen field.

17) Teachers must communicate clearly with their students.

      Teachers must communicate clearly with students.

18) People should be judged on their actions, not their appearance.

      People should be judged on actions, not appearance.

Application & Enrichment

Writing a Conclusion

At this point in your academic career, you have probably been asked to write a paragraph, essay, or paper. You may have gotten lots of advice on how to write an introduction or how to structure your writing. But every time you write something, consider whether you need to have a conclusion. For a short work of a couple of paragraphs, a concluding sentence may be appropriate, but for longer essays, reports, or books, a concluding paragraph—or even chapter—is needed. Remember that the goal of good writing is to communicate your points clearly to your reader. A conclusion tells your reader what they have just read and is your final opportunity to make your point.

You have been practicing an easy way to write a conclusion in several of the Application & Enrichment activities: paraphrasing. For your conclusion, you will paraphrase yourself! Here's how:

1) Start with your introduction.

The best place to start when you are thinking about a conclusion is simple: at the beginning. In your introduction, you have told your reader what you are going to write about. Now, for your conclusion, you will remind them what they have read.

2) Restate your thesis and summarize your supporting points.

What was the main point of your writing? What do you hope your reader will take away with them? Just like you have learned, don't copy word for word.

3) Make your final argument.

This is your last chance to make sure your reader understands your point!

One style tip: avoid starting your conclusion with "In conclusion..." or anything like it. Try to make that clear without saying it.

Directions

Read the following introduction. Paraphrase it to write a conclusion that

1) restates the thesis statement.

2) summarizes the supporting points.

Answers will vary.

While many people believe that the ancient Egyptians worshipped cats, that is not correct. Cats shared the everyday life of Egyptians. They admired cats for many traits that they shared with the Egyptian gods. Cats can be very gentle but also very fierce. They are also graceful. These were traits that the gods also had. The Egyptians worshipped the gods, not the cats.

Subject-Verb Agreement

Lesson 15: Subject-Verb Agreement

Like nouns and pronouns, verbs have **number**, too. A singular noun as the subject of a sentence (**boy**) takes a singular verb (**runs**): **boy runs**. A plural noun as the subject (**boys**) takes a plural verb (**run**): **boys run**. This is a very simple rule to remember and usually not a problem at all, except in a few cases that can cause confusion.

1) When there are modifiers between the subject and verb

   Example: A **group** of demonstrators **was** picketing outside.

   If we are not able to recognize that **group** is the subject of the sentence, we might think that the subject is **demonstrators**, a plural noun that is part of a prepositional phrase modifying the subject. If **demonstrators** were the subject, it would need a plural verb (**were**). But **group**, the actual subject, is a singular noun and needs a singular verb (in this case **was**). You can identify the subject of the sentence by removing all of the modifiers. This can make it easier to see whether to use a singular or plural verb.

2) When the subject is an indefinite pronoun

   Examples: **Each** of the girls **is** an excellent student.

   Both of the girls **are** excellent students.

   Lesson 14 included a list of singular and plural pronouns. Think about what the pronoun represents. In the first sentence, **each** indicates that each girl individually is an excellent student. In the second, **both** groups the girls together. Another clue in each sentence is the case of the predicate nominative: in the first sentence, it is singular (**an excellent student**) vs. the second, which is plural (**excellent students**). Again, strip down the sentence by removing modifiers to determine what form of the verb is needed.

3) When singular subjects are joined by **or** or **nor**

   Conjunctions always *join* words, but they don't always *combine* them. One of the most common conjunctions, **and**, joins words. Look at the following sentence:

   Example: The customer **and** the clerk **are** right. (*Two people are right.*)

   And *combines* the singular subjects **the customer** and **the clerk** into a **plural** subject that requires a **plural** verb (**are**).

   In contrast, **either/or** and **neither/nor** (or **or** and **nor** by themselves) do not combine subjects; the subjects are still separate entities. Therefore, if there are two singular subjects, the sentence will need a singular verb.

   Examples: **Neither** the customer **nor** the clerk **is** right. (*The customer is not right. The clerk is not right.*)

   Either the customer **or** the clerk **is** right. (*One person is right.*)

   Note: This rule is only true when **both** subjects are singular! If a singular subject and a plural subject are joined by **or** or **nor**, the verb agrees with the subject closest to it.

   Examples: Either my uncle or my cousins are coming for a visit.

   Either my **cousins** or my **uncle is** coming for a visit.

4) When the subject and verb are inverted

When a sentence begins with *here, there, where, when, why,* or *how,* be sure that the verb agrees with the subject. Sentences beginning with these words are often **inverted** sentences, with the subject coming after the verb. You will need to find the subject and make sure that the verb agrees with it.

Examples: There **are** two **athletes** in this race.

When **is** the **curtain** going up?

How **is** the **team** handling the new rule?

How **are** the **players** handling the new rule?

Subject-Verb Agreement: Exercise A

Directions

Circle the subject of each sentence below, then underline the correct verb.

1) (Cells) in your brain (needs, <u>need</u>) oxygen.

2) Our (players,) in position at the line of scrimmage, (was, <u>were</u>) awaiting the snap.

3) (Broadway,) with its flashing lights and bright colors, (<u>impresses</u>, impress) a visitor.

4) A (change) in the rules often (confuse, <u>confuses</u>) the spectators.

5) The (silence) inside the Carlsbad Caverns (<u>is</u>, are) awe-inspiring.

6) There (is, <u>are</u>) many vacation (destinations) to choose from.

7) Where (was, <u>were</u>) your (ancestors) from?

8) The (flowers) in the garden at the back of my house (is, <u>are</u>) beautiful in arrangements.

9) The (crowd) at the homecoming game (<u>was</u>, were) in excellent spirits.

10) These (exercises) on how to punctuate English (is, <u>are</u>) not that difficult.

Directions

Rewrite the following sentences, changing the conjunction **and** to **or** and vice versa. Change the verb to agree with the new situation.

Example: Ned and Larry have gone to the science fair.

*Either Ned **or** Larry **has** gone to the science fair.*

11) Either rain or snow has been predicted for tomorrow.

Rain and snow have been predicted for tomorrow.

12) Either John or Maria has prepared lunch.

John and Maria have prepared lunch.

13) The car in front of us and the car on the other side of the street are to blame.

Either the car in front of us or the car on the other side of the street is to blame.

14) The house on the hill and the cottage in the valley are for sale.

Either the house on the hill or the cottage in the valley is for sale.

15) Either Pumpkin or Lucky needs to have their nails trimmed.

Both Pumpkin and Lucky need to have their nails trimmed.

Subject-Verb Agreement: Exercise B

Directions

Circle the subject of each sentence below, then underline the correct verb.

1) (Many) of us (<u>like</u>, likes) long books.

2) There (is, <u>are</u>) many (reasons) why I can't go.

3) (Somebody) among the spectators (<u>was</u>, were) snoring.

4) (Has, <u>Have</u>) all of the (senators) returned?

5) (Nobody) in my family (<u>is</u>, are) able to remember phone numbers.

6) (Have, <u>Has</u>) (either) of you been to Mexico before?

7) Where (is, <u>are</u>) the (ingredients) for this recipe?

8) (Each) of the girls (<u>was</u>, were) eligible for the award.

9) (People) in the position in which you find yourself often (<u>try</u>, tries) to find new jobs.

10) The (author) who had written all those books (don't, <u>doesn't</u>) like to sign autographs.

Directions

Rewrite the following sentences, changing the conjunction **and** to **or** and vice versa. Change the verb to agree with the new situation.

11) Venus and Mars do not seem far away when you consider the vast distances of outer space.

   Venus or Mars does not seem far away when you consider the vast distances of outer space.

12) Each week a poem and an essay appear in the school newspaper.

   Each week a poem or an essay appears in the school newspaper.

13) Both the boy in the third row and the girl at the door have been called to the office.

   Either the boy in the third row or the girl at the door has been called to the office.

14) Either my uncle or my father-in-law was in Dallas when Kennedy was shot.

   My uncle and my father-in-law were in Dallas when Kennedy was shot.

15) Both my brother and my sister have graduated *magna cum laude*.

   Either my brother or my sister has graduated magna cum laude.

Application & Enrichment
Phrasal Verbs

By this point in the program, you know quite a bit about many different kinds of phrases and clauses. Earlier in this level, we talked about **phrasal adjectives**, or two or more words that are considered one modifier. There are also **phrasal verbs**, and they are built the same way: two or more words that act as a single verb.

Examples: **To catch:** to take hold or capture

> I caught the baseball before it could go over the fence.

To catch up: to move fast enough to draw even with someone ahead of you

> Hassan trailed in the race for several laps, but slowly he began to catch up.

To catch on: to understand

> I couldn't follow the game's rules, but I started to catch on.

To catch at: to snag

> The briars caught at my sweater and tore a stitch.

To catch out: to expose a wrongdoing

> When I tried to sneak an extra brownie, Stella caught me out.

While these aren't complete definitions, they show that these verbs all mean very different things. Yet, without the preposition, they wouldn't mean different things at all. (Remember way back in Level 3 when you learned about words that look like prepositions but are really adverbs?* That's because they are part of a phrasal verb!)

*Refer to your notes from Level 3 on prepositions and adverbs if needed.

A phrasal verb is not simply a verb followed by a preposition. The combination of words, much like a phrasal adjective, gives a specific meaning to the phrase. There are a couple of guidelines for their use:

- Don't try to combine prepositions. The phrasal verb has a specific meaning, and adding another preposition to it can be confusing.

> *phrasal prepositional*
> *verb   phrase*
>
> Don't <u>fill up</u> (on snacks) (before dinner)!

not

> *   prepositional*
> *verb   phrase*
>
> Don't fill (upon snacks) (before dinner)!

If you combine the words, you may lose the preposition that gives your phrasal verb its specific meaning.

- There may be words between the parts of a phrasal verb.

> We went through our closets and *gave* a lot of things *away*.

> I make sure to *put* my seatbelt *on* as soon as I get into the car.

- Phrasal verbs do not have hyphens. When you are using a phrasal verb, make sure you write the words separately.

    build up, not *build-up*

While these phrases are written separately when they are used as verbs, they are often (not always!) written as one word if they are used as nouns.

Phrasal Verb	Compound Noun
spin off	spinoff
build up	buildup
work out	workout
melt down	meltdown
hold up	holdup

Directions

Find the phrasal verb in the sentence. If it is incorrect, write it correctly in the space. If it is correct, write **correct**.

1) Because of the weather, we had to call-off the baseball game. _____
    call off

2) Beverly filled her glass upto the very top. _____
    filled up

3) Please look through the refrigerator and throw anything old or expired away. _____
    throw away

4) Laura waited on a lot of tables tonight! _____
    correct

5) I hope I have the energy to workout after work. _____
    work out

6) If you will see to the dishes afterwards, I will make dinner. _____
    correct

7) Juan was let-down by the movie made from his favorite book. _____
    let down

8) We got away with being late to class because the professor was not there yet. _____
    correct

9) The caterers will cleanup before they leave the reception. _____
    clean up

10) I ended-up near the lake instead of the park. _____
    ended up

Lesson 16: Which Pronoun?

Some rules for choosing which pronoun to use or how to list multiple subjects are as simple as understanding the grammar behind them. Others are based on rules of etiquette.

1) When using the personal pronouns *I* or *me* with another noun or pronoun, always **put the other guy first**. Just as you might hold the door open for someone else and let them go through first, list them first in the compound situation.

Examples: Incorrect: He told **me and Jim** to return after lunch.

Correct: He told **Jim and me** to return after lunch.

Incorrect: **Mila, I, and Beth** all made the team.

Correct: **Mila, Beth, and I** all made the team.

2) When listing multiple people in a sentence, place them in "social" order by listing them from oldest to youngest whenever possible. Just as you would show respect to an older person if you were with them in a social setting (for example, by allowing them to sit down first), list them first. This is a guideline based on good manners and not grammar, so do your best if you don't know the actual ages of the people who are listed.

Example: Incorrect: **My mom, my grandma, and I** went to brunch on Sunday.

Correct: **My grandma, my mom, and I** went to brunch on Sunday.

3) Which is correct: "Give this book to Bob or **I**," or "Give this book to Bob or **me**"? Would you say, "**We** girls had a great time," or "**Us** girls had a great time"?

It's possible to determine which pronoun should be used by taking out the rest of the group, leaving the pronoun and determining the job it is doing in the sentence:

Give this book to **I**.

Give this book to **me**.

Me is the correct choice because it is the object of the prepositional phrase *to me*. The objective case, *me*, is needed. What about the other example?

We had a great time.

Us had a great time.

We is the subject of the sentence, so the subjective case is needed.

What is the *case* of a pronoun?

Think about all of the jobs a noun can do: subject, direct object, indirect object, object of the preposition, and predicate nominative. Pronouns can do all of those same jobs, but unlike nouns, some pronouns change their form depending on the job they are doing. This is the **case** of the pronoun.

Case	Job or Use	Pronouns
Subjective (or Nominative)	• Subject • Predicate nominative	I, we, you, he, she, it, they, who, whoever
Objective	• Direct object • Indirect object • Object of the preposition	me, us, you, him, her, it, them, whom, whomever
Possessive	• Showing ownership	my/mine, our/ours, your/yours, his, her/hers, its, their/theirs, whose
Reflexive or Intensive	• Object of verb when subject and object are the same • Emphasize the subject or antecedent	myself, ourselves, yourself/yourselves, himself, herself, itself, themselves

About Reflexive and Intensive Pronouns

These pronouns are often misused, but the rules are not difficult to master, since they are used in quite specific situations.

Reflexive Pronouns

Use a reflexive pronoun when the subject of a sentence is the same as the object.

Examples: **Zahra** prepared dinner for **herself**.

Who is preparing dinner? **Zahra**—subject

Whom is dinner for? **for herself (Zahra)**—object of the preposition

Dad bought **himself** a new car.

Who bought a new car? **Dad**—subject

Whom did Dad buy a car for? **himself (Dad)**—indirect object

Intensive pronouns (or Intensifiers)

Use intensifiers when you want to emphasize the subject or antecedent.

Examples: **Zahra** prepared dinner **herself**. (No one helped Zahra; she prepared it on her own.)

Dad bought the new car **himself**. (Dad paid for the new car without help from anyone.)

Often, an intensifier is found right after its antecedent.

Examples: **The author herself** came to the opening night of the play.

No one is responsible for your actions but **you yourself**.

Reflexive and intensive pronouns should never be used in a sentence if there is no antecedent referring to the same person or thing.

Examples: Incorrect: Give the book to Bob or **myself**. (*Myself* is incorrect because neither *me* nor *I* is in the sentence as its antecedent.)

Correct: Give the book to Bob or **me**. (*Me* is correct, because it is the object of the preposition *to*.)

4) When a pronoun is used as a predicate nominative, use the subjective/nominative case. This situation is tricky, because in informal everyday speech, we use it incorrectly all the time!

Examples: The top student in the class was **me**.

The top student in the class was **I**.

Which sounds correct? Probably number one—but it isn't! Using what we've learned about grammar, we know that *was* is a linking verb, and that *student* (subject) and *I* (predicate nominative) are the same person. We could rewrite the sentence as follows:

I was the top student in the class.

When we rewrite it this way, we can easily see that we need to use the subjective case of the pronoun, also known as the nominative case.

This is another example of grammar that today is usually only found in formal writing. If we were talking or writing to our friends, "It was me" is perfectly acceptable even though technically incorrect. However, in formal written work (and grammar workbooks!), remember that pronouns used as predicate nominatives need to be in the subjective/nominative case: "It was I."

Which Pronoun?: Exercise A

Directions

Circle the correct pronoun in the parentheses. If the nouns and pronouns are in the wrong order, rewrite the noun phrase so that they are in the correct order. Choose the **correct** pronoun for formal usage, even if we don't use the correct pronoun in everyday speech.

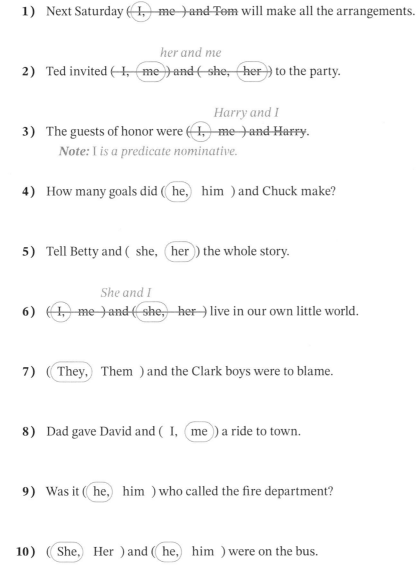

                    Tom and I

1) Next Saturday (I, me) and Tom will make all the arrangements.

                    her and me

2) Ted invited (I, me) and (she, her) to the party.

                         Harry and I

3) The guests of honor were (I, me) and Harry.
         Note: I *is a predicate nominative.*

4) How many goals did (he, him) and Chuck make?

5) Tell Betty and (she, her) the whole story.

             She and I

6) (I, me) and (she, her) live in our own little world.

7) (They, Them) and the Clark boys were to blame.

8) Dad gave David and (I, me) a ride to town.

9) Was it (he, him) who called the fire department?

10) (She, Her) and (he, him) were on the bus.

Directions

The following sentences are incorrect. Rewrite them to make them correct.

11) Me and Janie went to the mall yesterday.

Janie and I went to the mall yesterday.

12) Either Wendy, Jason, or myself will be there to make sure the doors are open.

Either Wendy, Jason, or I will be there to make sure the doors are open.

13) Please give your tickets to Julie, Crystal, or I.

Please give your tickets to Julie, Crystal, or me.

14) Me, my mom, and my grandma went to Gallo's for dinner.

My grandma, my mom, and I went to Gallo's for dinner.

15) Mrs. Phillips gave Bob and I a makeup test the next day.

Mrs. Phillips gave Bob and me a makeup test the next day.

Which Pronoun?: Exercise B

Directions

Circle the correct pronoun in the parentheses. If the nouns and pronouns are in the wrong order, rewrite the noun phrase so that they are in the correct order. Choose the **correct** pronoun for formal usage, even if we don't use the correct pronoun in everyday speech.

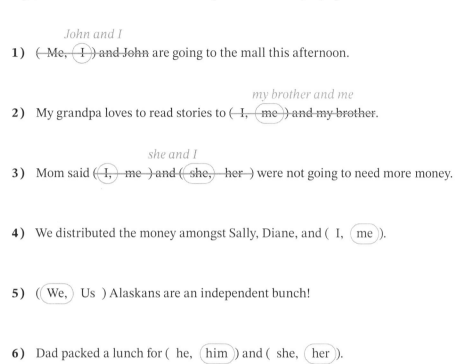

John and I

1) (Me, I) and John are going to the mall this afternoon.

my brother and me

2) My grandpa loves to read stories to (I, me) and my brother.

she and I

3) Mom said (I, me) and (she, her) were not going to need more money.

4) We distributed the money amongst Sally, Diane, and (I, me).

5) (We, Us) Alaskans are an independent bunch!

6) Dad packed a lunch for (he, him) and (she, her).

Bev and me

7) Will you help (I, me) and Bev clean the recreation room?

8) Jerome wrote a poem to (we, us) students in the senior class.

9) (She, Her) and (I, me) will join you later for lunch.

10) Mr. Wilson gave (he, him) and (I, me) a few pointers about football.

Directions

The following sentences are incorrect. Rewrite them to make them correct.

11) Mr. Bates gave a copy of the Winners' List to Mrs. Sampson and myself.

Mr. Bates gave a copy of the Winners' List to Mrs. Sampson and me.

12) Either Erin or myself will see you later.

Either Erin or I will see you later.

13) Me, my uncle, and my grandpa went to Disney World last summer.

My grandpa, my uncle, and I went to Disney World last summer.

14) Him and John were the ones who had their notes typed.

He and John were the ones who had their notes typed.

15) My brother, my grandpa, me, and my dad all went to the baseball game last night.

My grandpa, my dad, my brother, and I all went to the baseball game last night.

Application & Enrichment
Email Etiquette

Do you remember how we often point out rules that you should follow in formal writing? We're going to describe one of those formal writing situations and give you some handy pointers!

At some point in your life, you will find yourself needing to write a formal email, whether to a professor, an employer, or a business. While you may be able to communicate the same thing in informal slang, you will be taken more seriously and viewed more professionally if you can communicate in an appropriate, formal manner.

Formal writing doesn't have to be stuffy or impersonal. It means considering your audience and treating them appropriately. If you wouldn't walk up to your principal or doctor and say, "Dude, what's up?", then you shouldn't say that in written communication, either. For business, school, or work communication, use your best manners. Not only is it the right thing to do, but you're also more likely to get a positive response.

- Use an appropriate greeting. *Dear* might seem pretty old fashioned these days, but it is always a safe choice. You can also use *hello, hi,* or simply the person's name with the proper courtesy title, depending on the situation and your relationship with the person. But make sure you include something—don't just dive right into your email:

    Dear Dr. Watson,

    Hello, Ms. Heffelfinger,

    Hi, Professor Murgatroyd,

    Senator Muddel,

    You will need a comma after *Hi* or *Hello* (but not *Dear*) and a comma after their name.

- Put the topic of your question in the subject line of the email. Consider including your name as well—businesses and professors deal with a lot of people, so knowing *who* is asking *what* increases your chance of getting a quick response. This is an especially good idea if you have an email address that doesn't include your name.

- Get right to the point. Put the main topic of your question or information in the first sentence, and include your name.

- Use complete sentences. Fragments can be distracting.

- Use your manners. *Please* and *thank you* go a long way, especially when you are asking for something!

- Don't use texting shorthand. Using expressions like IDK or HBU may save time, but it's not worth it if your recipient doesn't take you seriously or doesn't understand you.

- Check your spelling and grammar. Remember, you want to be taken seriously.

- Use an appropriate closing. *Sincerely* or *Thank you* are both great options.

- Give your name again after the closing.

Almost all of these suggestions, with the exception of the subject line, can also be applied to writing a letter. Good written communication skills must be learned, but they are important and will serve you well for the rest of your life.

Directions

Choose the best option. Circle the letter of your answer.

1) Pick the best subject for an email from a student to a professor.

    A) Hey quick question

    B) Question about ENGL101 writing assignment—Smith

    C) Question about ENGL101 writing assignment

    D) Question about ENGL101

2) Pick the best greeting for an email to someone you don't know well.

    A) Dear Dr. Watson,

    B) Hey Doc,

    C) Hi.

    D) None. Get straight to the point.

3) Pick the best opening sentence.

    A) How are you?

    B) I have a request to make, and I hope you will consider it.

    C) idk what to do.

    D) This is Jenn Smith and I have a question about the writing assignment for ENGL101.

4) Choose the best closing for the email.

    A) Later,
        Jenn Smith

    B) Ciao,
        Jenn

    C) Thx

    D) Thank you for your time,
        Jenn Smith

Directions

There are five errors in the following email. Some are etiquette errors and others are grammar or usage errors. How many can you find? Cross out errors and correct them or write what is wrong below the sentence.

Hey Mr. Jimenez,
1   *2*

                    your
What's up? I need ~~ur~~ help with class. I'm stuck.
      3   *4*

See you later
~~CU l8r~~,
   5

Geoff Drew

Answers may vary, but some possible errors are indicated. Students may also point out that Geoff did not provide details about his question or identify himself in the first sentence.

1: greeting

2: missing comma

3: don't start with small talk

4: text slang

5: text slang

Usage Assessment, Lessons 13–15

Remember to look at the lesson notes if you need help with any section.

Pronoun-Antecedent Agreement

Directions

Circle the correct pronoun.

Correct answers are worth one point each.

_____ **1)** Neither Bill nor Mark had told me which color (⟨he,⟩ they) wanted.
 1

_____ **2)** I had to read each of the essays carefully before I could grade (⟨it,⟩ them).
 1

_____ **3)** Jim and Mike will lend us (his, ⟨their⟩) history notes.
 1

_____ **4)** If someone makes the effort, (he, ⟨they,⟩ you) can usually accomplish a goal.
 1

_____ **5)** I feel that cleaning (⟨my,⟩ your, one's) room is my least favorite chore.
 1

═══
 5

Directions

Write the correct pronoun in the blank space.

Correct answers are worth one point each.

_____ **6)** Angelo and Mario will attend with _____ parents.
 1   *their*

_____ **7)** Either Tim or Tyler will sponsor _____ own team this year.
 1   *his*

_____ **8)** Neither Ray nor Brad will do _____ homework alone.
 1   *his*

_____ **9)** Is either Beth or Betsy going to read _____ essay aloud?
 1   *her*

___**10)** Neither this dish nor that plate is in _____ regular place on the shelf.
_1_   *its*

___**11)** Either Mr. Marley or Mr. Engels parked _____ car in the driveway.
_1_   *his*

___**12)** Did either Earl or Dave turn in _____ book report early?
_1_   *his*

___**13)** Both Wes and Paul came to run _____ laps on the track.
_1_   *their*

___**14)** Should Al and Jane call _____ parents before we begin?
_1_   *their*

___**15)** Neither Sarah nor Marian wants _____ name to be called.
_1_   *her*

___
_10_

Subject-Verb Agreement

Directions

Circle the correct verb.

Correct answers are worth one point each.

___**16)** John, as well as some of the other club members, ((plans,) plan) to ask questions.
_1_

___**17)** As each one of you students (know, (knows)), your reports will be due on Friday.
_1_

___**18)** There (is, (are)) some leftover sandwiches in the refrigerator.
_1_

___**19)** Nobody in my family ((is,) are) any good at video games.
_1_

___**20)** (Has, (Have)) all of the team members suited up?
_1_

___
_5_

Directions
Read the sentences below carefully. If the verb agrees with its subject, write **Y** in the space. If it does not agree, write the correct verb in the space.

Correct answers are worth one point each.

Y	**21)**	One of the cabinets contains the club's banner and membership rolls.
is	**22)**	Each of the hostesses are standing in the doorway.
were	**23)**	The numbers on the license plate was covered with mud.
has	**24)**	Every one of the clerks have to punch the time clock.
Y	**25)**	The bridges on Highway 34 are extremely narrow.
answers	**26)**	One of the assistants answer the telephone.
covers	**27)**	Our assignment for the next two days cover events during the French Revolution.
stands	**28)**	A bag of golf clubs, as well as two tennis rackets, stand in the corner of the closet.
Y	**29)**	Each of the farmers uses modern machines.
Y	**30)**	Does either of the girls play the piano?

10

Directions

Rewrite each sentence by following the directions in the parentheses and changing the verb accordingly.

Correct answers are worth one point each.

Example: The boys have finished delivering the papers. (*Change **the boys** to **each of the boys***)

Each of the boys has finished delivering the papers.

___ **31)** My sister is planning to attend summer school. (*Change **sister** to **sisters***)

1   *My sisters are planning to attend summer school.*

___ **32)** Nobody in our town intends to participate in the ceremony. (*Change **Nobody** to **Many***)

1   *Many in our town intend to participate in the ceremony.*

___ **33)** Most of the money was contributed by children. (*Change **money** to **quarters***)

1   *Most of the quarters were contributed by children.*

___ **34)** Neither the students nor the teacher has found the missing book. (*Remove **Neither***

1   *and change **nor** to **and***)

The students and the teacher have found the missing book.

___ **35)** Some of the workers spend too much time in the snack bar. (*Change **Some** to **One**.*)

1   *One of the workers spends too much time in the snack bar.*

═══
5

Directions

Circle the correct pronoun in the parentheses. If the nouns and pronouns are in the wrong order, rewrite the noun phrase so that they are in the correct order. Choose the **correct** pronoun for formal usage, even if we don't use the correct pronoun in everyday speech.

him and me

____ **36)** The accident taught (~~I,~~ me) and (~~he,~~ him) a lesson.
_3_

her and me

____ **37)** The waiter asked (~~I,~~ me) and (~~she,~~ her) what we wanted.
_3_

Jack and me

____ **38)** Have you been avoiding (~~I,~~ me) and ~~Jack~~?
_2_

____ **39)** Have you and (her, she) had an argument?
_1_

____ **40)** It was (he, him) who called the police.
_1_

____ **41)** Is it (she, her) whom you are marrying?
_1_

Ben and me

____ **42)** Sam helped (~~I,~~ me) ~~and Ben~~ paint the garage.
_2_

____ **43)** I haven't heard a word from either Judith or (her, she).
_1_

____ **44)** The letters are for you, Paula, and (I, me).
_1_

Frank and me

____ **45)** Please give (~~I,~~ me) ~~and Frank~~ another chance.
_2_

___ **46)** He rode his bike between (~~I,~~ (me)) ~~and Clara~~.
Clara and me

2

___ **47)** The job of buying refreshments was assigned to (~~I,~~ (me)) ~~and Jerry~~.
Jerry and me

2

___ **48)** You have to choose between (~~I,~~ (me)) and (~~she,~~ (her)).
her and me

3

___ **49)** ((We,) Us) three have to sing the solo parts.

1

___ **50)** (~~Me,~~ (I)), ~~Mom, and Grandma~~ all went on the Ferris wheel.
Grandma, Mom, and I

2

——
27

=== *Total Points* $\dfrac{50}{62} = 80\%$
62

Who or Whom?

Lesson 17: Who or Whom?

Correctly using **who** and **whom** or **whoever** and **whomever** is a skill that can set grammar masters apart from the crowd. Like a couple of other examples of proper grammar we've mentioned, this is a rule that is often overlooked in everyday, informal speech. In your writing for school or work, however, using them correctly shows that you understand the structure of a sentence you are using and can add to your credibility as a writer.

To know whether to use **who** or **whom**, look at the sentence and identify what job the pronoun is doing in the sentence. With practice, choosing the correct pronoun will become second nature.

Who and **whoever** are used when the pronoun is acting as a **subject** or **predicate nominative**. That's why this case is called the **subjective** or **nominative case**.

Whom and **whomever** are used when the pronoun is being an **object** (direct object, indirect object, or object of the preposition). This case is called the **objective case**.

Here's a shortcut: Look at the question being asked by these interrogative pronouns. If the answer to the question could be **he**, use **who**. If the answer could be **him**, use **whom**.

Examples: To **whom** are you speaking? (**whom** is the *object* of the preposition)

Who are those men? (**Who** is the *subject* of the verb **are**)

Whom was the speaker attacking? (**Whom** is the direct *object* of **attacking**)

Whoever wishes to come is welcome. (**Whoever** is the *subject* of the verb **is**)

We did not know **whom** the man wanted. (**whom** is the direct *object* of **wanted**)

John is the boy **who** needs your help. (**who** is the *subject* of **needs**)

Don't be misled by interrupters such as "do you think," "shall I say," or "do you suppose." Remove them from the sentence if it helps determine which pronoun to use.

Examples: Who do you suppose will be elected? (**Who** is the *subject* of **will be elected**)

Whom do you think he meant? (**Whom** is the direct *object* of **meant**)

Who shall I say is calling? (**Who** is the *subject* of **is calling**)

One way to quickly identify what job the pronoun is doing in a sentence is to match up all the subjects and verbs in the sentence. Find all the verbs and look for their subjects. If you find a verb without a subject, the pronoun **who** is probably it. Watch out for linking verbs—because **who** could be a predicate nominative! If it's not the subject of a verb, it's probably an object and it should be **whom**.

Who and Whom: Exercise A

Directions

Circle the correct pronoun in the parentheses. In the space provided below each sentence, write what job it's doing. If it's a subject, write the verb that it's the subject of. If it's an object, write which word it is the object of.

1) (Who, (Whom)) did you see at the game?

Whom *is the direct object of* did see

2) He is the one (who, (whom)) we least suspected.

whom *is the direct object of* suspected

3) To (who, (whom)) did you submit your application?

whom *is the object of the preposition* to

4) Please support ((whoever,) whomever) is elected.

whoever *is the subject of* is elected

5) I shall support (whoever, (whomever)) the class chooses.

whomever *is the direct object of* chooses

6) (Whom, (Who)) do you think will win the election?

Who *is the subject of* will win

7) We nominated candidates ((who,) whom) we thought would win.

who *is the subject of* would win

8) From (who, (whom)) did you get that information?

whom *is the object of the preposition* from

9) (Whoever, (Whomever)) he sees, Sam says "hello" to them.

Whomever *is the direct object of* sees

10) ((Whoever,) Whomever) wants to come, the door is open.

Whoever *is the subject of* wants

Who and Whom: Exercise B

Directions

Circle the correct pronoun in the parentheses. In the space provided below each sentence, write what job it's doing. If it's a subject, write the verb that it's the subject of. If it's an object, write which word it is the object of.

1) Most of the people ((who,) whom) are hired live within 30 miles.

who *is the subject of* are hired

2) Most of the people (who, (whom)) they hire live within 30 miles.

whom *is the direct object of* hire

3) Give this report to ((whoever,) whomever) is in the office.

whoever *is the subject of* is

4) (Who, (Whom)) do you need to see, Mrs. Jones?

Whom *is the direct object of* to see

5) ((Who,) Whom) do you suppose is the winner of the contest?

Who *is the subject of* is

6) I don't remember (who, (whom)) you want to invite.

whom *is the direct object of* to invite

7) ((Who,) Whom) do you think called the police?

Who *is the subject of* called

8) Do you know (who, (whom)) the police suspect?

whom *is the direct object of* suspect

9) (Who, (Whom)) do you want to speak to?

Whom *is the object of the preposition* to

10) She is the one (who, (whom)) we must stop.

whom *is the direct object of* must stop

Application & Enrichment
Assorted Usage Errors

Good and well

Good is an adjective. It describes a noun. *Well* is an adverb; it describes an adverb, adjective, or verb.

Examples: I am having a **good** day. (*good* modifies the noun *day*)

My day is going **well**. (*well* modifies the verb *is going*)

Some people who are familiar with this rule could be annoyed if they ask "How are you?" and you reply, "I'm good!" In their minds, not only did you technically not answer their question, but you have also boldly claimed that you are a good person! (You might very well be one, but many people believe that humility is a part of being a good person. And it's not very humble to go around telling people you are good!) This is another example of a rule that is often broken in informal speech but that you should be aware of for formal writing.

Fewer and less

Fewer is a plural modifier. It modifies **count nouns**, or things that can be counted; for example, **one cat**, **two cats**, **three cats**, and so on. If there aren't as many cats, you would say *fewer cats*. Count nouns can be singular or plural.

Less is a singular modifier. It modifies **noncount nouns**, or things that cannot be counted. For example, you can't count **one sand**, **two sands**, **three sands**... It's a noncount noun: **sand**. If there is not as much sand, you would say *less sand*. Nouns that are measured by volume are noncount nouns. Noncount nouns are always singular.

Examples: Jack had **fewer colds** this winter. (*Can you count* **colds***?*)

There is **less snow** this year than last year. (*Can you count* **snow***?*)

There are **fewer inches** of snow this year than last year. (*Can you count* **inches***?*)

This product contains **less fat**. (*Can you count* **fat***?*)

There are **fewer grams** of fat in this one. (*Can you count* **grams***?*)

This cheese has **fewer calories**. (*Can you count* **calories***?*)

Double negatives

If you say, "I didn't do nothing," what are you really saying? If you didn't do **nothing**, that means you did do **something**! Double negatives cancel each other out and become a positive. Be on the lookout for words that have a negative meaning beyond *not*, *never*, and *nothing*. *Hardly*, *barely*, and *scarcely* are examples of negative words that shouldn't be used with another negative. "There *wasn't hardly* anyone on the tennis court," is incorrect and actually means that there were a lot of people on the tennis court. The correct way to say this is, "There **was hardly** anyone on the tennis court.

Should of, would of, could of

This is caused by confusion based on how the contractions **should've** (**should have**), **would've** (**would have**) and **could've** (**could have**) sound when they are spoken. It sounds like **should of** when you say **should've** (try it!), but what you are really saying is **should have**.

Directions
Find the double negatives in the following sentences, and cross one out to make the sentence correct.
Try to fix the sentence by only crossing something out and not by rewriting it.

1) We couldn't hardly hear the speaker.

2) The car didn't stop for no stoplights.

3) Connie hadn't never flown in an airplane.

or Connie hadn't never flown in an airplane.

4) The injured horse couldn't barely walk.

5) Seniors don't have nothing to complain about.

Directions
Circle the correct word in parentheses to complete the sentence.

6) The ending of the book was really ((good,) well)!

7) Ted had ((fewer,) less) first-place votes than George.

8) My grandfather was very ill, but he is (good, (well)) now.

9) Next time you bake a cake, use ((fewer,) less) eggs.

10) Next time you bake a cake, use (fewer, (less)) vanilla.

Directions

If there is a usage error in the sentence, cross it out and write the correct answer in the blank. If there are no errors, write **correct**.

11) You ~~should of~~ seen that movie!

_____
should've or *should have*

12) I wish you ~~would of~~ gone to the party.

_____
would've or *would have*

13) We ~~could of~~ gone to see Taylor Swift, but we couldn't get tickets.

_____
could've or *could have*

14) I could've been a contender!

_____
correct

15) Dad wishes he ~~wouldn't of~~ had that fifth slice of pizza.

_____
wouldn't have

(**Note:** *if your student didn't include* n't *when they cross out the incorrect answer, the correct answer is* would have)

Adjective or Adverb?

Lesson 18: Adjective or Adverb?

Another habit that will showcase your good grammar skills is to use **adjectives** and **adverbs** correctly.

Example: That dress fits **perfect**.

That dress fits **perfectly**.

The word *perfect* is an adjective, so it must modify a noun, as in *a perfect fit* or *the perfect dress*. In the first sentence above, however, it is used to try to describe how the dress *fits*. *Fits* is a verb, so it must be modified with an adverb, *perfectly*.

Be careful when a sentence includes a linking verb! There may be a predicate adjective, in which case you don't want an adverb.

Example: That dress is **perfect**. (*perfect* is a predicate adjective describing the noun *dress*)

That dress is **perfectly**. (*perfectly* is an adverb and sounds silly here!)

People seem to have a lot of difficulty choosing whether to use the adjectives *good* and *bad* or the adverbs *well* and *badly*.

- *Good* and *bad* are adjectives that either modify nouns or complete linking verbs.

   Example: The day was **good** (or **bad**) for a picnic. (*good* modifies the noun *day*)

- *Well* and *badly* are adverbs that modify verbs or other modifiers.

   Example: He did **well** (or **badly**) on the test. (*well* modifies the verb *did*)

Note: *well* can be used as an adjective if you are using it to mean "in good health."

Examples: Mrs. Thatcher does not look **well** today.

(*Mrs. Thatcher does not look **in good health** today.*)

I haven't felt **well** for several days.

(*I haven't felt **in good health** for several days.*)

Adjective or Adverb?: Exercise A

Directions

Circle the correct word in the parentheses. In the space provided following each sentence, write either **adjective** or **adverb** and what is being modified. If it's a predicate adjective, write **predicate adjective** and the linking verb.

1) You can finish the job (easy, (easily)) in an hour.

 adverb modifying can finish

2) The sky remained ((clear,) clearly) all day long.

 predicate adjective of remained

3) The mechanic stayed (steady, (steadily)) on the job until it was finished.

 adverb modifying stayed

4) The rancher seemed ((uneasy,) uneasily) about the weather bureau's storm warning.

 predicate adjective of seemed

5) Mary felt ((unhappy,) unhappily) about her report card.

 predicate adjective of felt

Directions

If the capitalized word is incorrect in the sentence below, cross it out and write the correct word. If the sentence is correct, write **correct**.

6) Harry sounded ~~ANGRILY~~ on the phone.

 angry

7) The repair job was done ~~CAREFUL~~.

 carefully

8) The left shoe now seemed to fit ~~PERFECT~~.

 perfectly

9) Football is played DIFFERENTLY in Canada.

 correct

10) Janelle gazed ~~UNHAPPY~~ at her ruined dress.

 unhappily

Adjective or Adverb?: Exercise B

Directions

Circle the correct word in the parentheses. In the space provided following each sentence, write either **adjective** or **adverb** and what is being modified. If it's a predicate adjective, write **predicate adjective** and the linking verb.

1) Doris picked up her purse (quick, (quickly)), threw on a coat, and ran out the door.

adverb modifying picked

2) You can run a small car more (economical, (economically)) than a large one.

adverb modifying can run

3) The poem sounds ((different,) differently) in French.

predicate adjective of sounds

4) Mark's knee was hurt (bad, (badly)) during the first game.

adverb modifying was hurt

5) Students should talk (quieter, (more quietly)) in the halls during classes.

adverb modifying should talk

Directions

If the capitalized word is incorrect in the sentence below, cross it out and write the correct word. If the sentence is correct, write **correct**.

6) Stir the mixture ~~GOOD~~ before adding the milk.

well

7) Carolyn did ~~BAD~~ on the exam.

badly

8) Be sure to mix the sand and cement ~~GOOD~~.

well

9) You can see just as WELL from the balcony.

correct

10) Harriet feels ~~BADLY~~ about losing your earring.

bad (feels is a linking verb)

Application & Enrichment
Paraphrasing

Directions
Parse and diagram the first line of this poem. Then paraphrase the poem.

"I, Too"
by Langston Hughes

pro adv   av   pn
I, too, sing America.

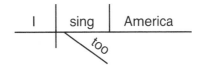

I am the darker brother.
They send me to eat in the kitchen
When company comes,
But I laugh,
And eat well,
And grow strong.

Tomorrow,
I'll be at the table
When company comes.
Nobody'll dare
Say to me,
"Eat in the kitchen,"
Then.

Besides,
They'll see how beautiful I am
And be ashamed—
I, too, am America.

Active and Passive Voice

Lesson 19: Active and Passive Voice

Active voice and **passive voice** are terms you will hear a lot when you write. It's important to know what each term means and when each is appropriate. Most of the time, active voice is preferred, so it's also important to know how to change a passive sentence into an active sentence.

Active voice

In sentences written in **active voice**, the **subject** is the **doer** that is performing the **action of the verb**. Here are some sentences that show active voice:

Examples: The **boy threw** the ball. (*boy is the subject/doer;* ***threw*** *is the action*)

My **mother sings** beautifully. (***mother*** *is the subject/doer;* ***sings*** *is the action*)

Watch your step. (*The understood* ***you*** *is the subject/doer;* ***watch*** *is the action*)

As mentioned, active voice is generally preferred in most writing because it makes your writing more vivid and clear. The reader doesn't have to do any mental gymnastics to figure out who or what is doing what action.

Passive voice

A sentence in **passive voice** has the **object** of an action acting as the **subject**. Here are passive versions of the sentences above:

Examples: The **ball was thrown** by the boy. (***ball*** *is the subject;* ***was thrown*** *is the action;* ***boy*** *is the doer*)

A **song was** beautifully **sung** by my mother. (***song*** *is the subject;* ***was sung*** *is the action;* ***mother*** *is the doer*)

Steps should be taken carefully. (***steps*** *is the subject;* ***should be taken*** *is the action; understood* ***you*** *is the doer*)

Passive voice generally requires more words to make the subject, doer, and action clear than active voice does. Sometimes the doer that is performing the action is not included in the sentence at all! It's easy to see why this could be less clear to a reader. Look at the first two example sentences rewritten to leave out the doer:

Examples: The **ball was thrown**. (***ball*** *is the subject;* ***was thrown*** *is the action;* **???** *is the doer*)

A **song was** beautifully **sung**. (***song*** *is the subject;* ***was sung*** *is the action;* **???** *is the doer*)

Spotting the passive voice

Passive voice can be spotted... (wait! That's passive voice! Let's try again...)

You can spot passive voice by looking for this verb construction:

form of ***to be*** + past participle

To be forms include *are, am, is, was, were, has been, had been, will be, will have been,* and so on. There may be helping verbs and modals, such as *can be, would be,* and *might have been,* for example.

Another hint to identifying passive voice is if the sentence ends with a prepositional phrase including *by*. If the doer is included in a passive voice sentence, they are usually put at the end of the sentence as the object of the prepositional phrase. You can see this in the first two sentences given as examples under the definition of **passive voice**, above. Here are a couple more passive voice sentences with this construction:

Examples: The exercise was written **by the teacher**.

The test was taken **by the student**.

In both of these sentences, the doer of the action is not the subject, but is instead found in the prepositional phrase at the end of the sentence.

Is passive voice always wrong, then?

Not at all. It should be avoided most of the time, but there are some specific situations in which it's necessary or appropriate. There are times when you want to put the emphasis on the object rather than the subject. Let's say you were writing a murder mystery, the murder having taken place in a hotel room. The forensics team is there looking for clues. The following sentence:

The room had been cleaned by the housekeeper an hour prior to the murder..

is preferable to

The housekeeper had cleaned the room an hour prior to the murder.

because you might not want to draw attention to the housekeeper as a character in your story.

Or another example: let's say you are writing an obituary. The sentence

The body was interred at Forest Lawn Cemetery.

is more sensitive to the surviving loved ones than

The gravediggers interred the body at Forest Lawn Cemetery.

Perhaps the doer is unknown:

A crime was committed.

The last green popsicle was eaten.

The cave paintings were drawn many centuries ago.

Scientific and medical reports often use the passive voice to place the emphasis on the experiment or process rather than the doer:

The substance **was dissolved** in water. (The reader knows that *I* dissolved the substance; no need to say it.)

A bandage **was applied** to the wound. (It doesn't matter *who* applied the bandage, only that it was applied.)

Corporations, politicians, and other savvy communicators often use passive voice to shape the way a message is received. Because it's easy to leave the doer out of a passive sentence, some people use the passive voice to avoid mentioning who is responsible for certain actions:

Examples: The Acme Oil Company announced that a few gallons of oil might have been spilled. (*Oh, really? By whom?*)

Mistakes were made. (*"Mistakes were made...by someone. Maybe by us, maybe not. Carry on. Nothing to see here."*)

"Mom, the car was driven into a ditch." (*Shhh...maybe she won't figure it out!*)

There may be instances where you don't want the doer to be known:

Example: A large donation was made to the animal shelter. (*If the donor doesn't want to be named, this is one way to keep their anonymity.*)

In summary, use active voice whenever possible unless you have a purpose for obscuring the doer of an action.

Active & Passive Voice: Exercise A

Directions

Identify whether each sentence is active or passive by writing **A** (active) or **P** (passive) in the space provided next to each sentence.

A   **1)** The man painted the room a bright shade of blue.

P   **2)** The book was put on the shelf.

P   **3)** Cars were made on the factory line by the workers.

A   **4)** I bought a brand new car this weekend.

A   **5)** We've all made mistakes.

P   **6)** Errors were made along the way.

P   **7)** The results are being tabulated as we speak.

A   **8)** I'm writing a new book about my trials and tribulations in college.

P   **9)** The refrigerator was plugged into the wrong outlet.

P **10)** I am going to write my paper after lunch.

Directions

Now, in the space provided, rewrite the sentences above. If they are passive, rewrite them in the active voice. If they are active, rewrite them in the passive voice.

- Try to include all of the elements of the original sentence, although when you rewrite in passive voice, the doer may disappear from the sentence.

- Because passive voice sentences may not include the doer, you might need to invent a doer to be the subject of your new active voice sentence.

Answers will vary; one possible answer is provided.

11) *The room was painted a bright shade of blue.*

12) *I put the book on the shelf.*

13) *The workers made the cars on the factory line.*

14) *A new car was purchased this weekend.*

15) *Mistakes were made by all of us.*

16) *We made errors along the way.*

17) *Precinct workers are tabulating the results as we speak.*

18) *My trials and tribulations in college were written about in a new book.*

19) *I plugged the refrigerator into the wrong outlet.*

20) *My paper will be written after lunch.*

Active & Passive Voice: Exercise B

Directions

Identify whether each sentence is active or passive by writing *A* (active) or *P* (passive) in the space provided next to each sentence. Rewrite the sentence in the opposite voice on the lines provided.

Answers for rewritten sentences will vary; one possible answer is provided.

P **1)** At this evening's concert, selected famous arias will be sung by our star soprano.

    At this evening's concert, our star soprano will sing selected famous arias.

A **2)** Beginning tomorrow morning, workers will remove the windows.

    Beginning tomorrow morning, the windows will be removed by the workers.

P **3)** Although Melissa took great care in washing the dishes, a treasured wine glass was broken.

    Although she took great care in washing the dishes, Melissa broke a treasured wine glass.

P **4)** Using his smartphone, all of Brad's spring semester classes were chosen in one hour.

    Using his smartphone, Brad chose all of his spring semester classes in one hour.

P **5)** The packages were wrapped and taken to the post office by our shipping clerk yesterday.

    Our shipping clerk wrapped and took all the packages to the post office yesterday.

_A_ **6)** Using their state-of-the-art 3D glasses, the audience saw the new action thriller.

Using state-of-the-art 3D glasses, the new action thriller was seen by the audience.

_A_ **7)** The CEO and the vice president of operations planned all of next year's conventions.

All of next year's conventions were planned by the CEO and the vice president of operations.

_P_ **8)** The crumpled party dress was washed and ironed by the housekeeper before the next evening.

The housekeeper washed and ironed the crumpled party dress before the next evening.

_P_ **9)** While the fascinated science class watched, the secret ingredient was stirred into the mixture.

While the fascinated science class watched, the teacher stirred the secret ingredient into

the mixture.

_P_ **10)** By ten o'clock on the third day of their camping trip, the tents had been neatly packed away.

They had neatly packed away the tents by ten o'clock on the third day of their camping trip.

Active & Passive Voice: Exercise C

Directions

Identify whether each sentence is active or passive by writing **A** (active) or **P** (passive) in the space provided next to each sentence. Rewrite the sentence in the opposite voice on the lines provided.

Answers for rewritten sentences will vary; one possible answer is provided.

P **1)** Despite the massive public protests, the bill was passed by the Senate and the House.

Despite the massive public protests, the Senate and the House passed the bill.

P **2)** Even though the pitcher was trying to pitch a fair game, the batter was hit by a fastball.

Even though the pitcher was trying to pitch a fair game, he hit a batter with a fastball.

A **3)** Why did the chicken cross the road?

Why was the road crossed by the chicken?

A **4)** Even though Meg, Jo, Beth, and Amy didn't let on, they surprised Marmee with gifts.

Even though Meg, Jo, Beth, and Amy didn't let on, Marmee was surprised with gifts.

P **5)** Because it was the middle of the night, the kitty was taken to the emergency vet.

Because it was the middle of the night, I took the kitty to the emergency vet.

_A_ **6)** The outside consultant damaged many relationships in our office.

Many relationships in our office were damaged by the outside consultant.

_P_ **7)** A huge new marketing plan has been put into place in our company.

Our company has put a huge new marketing plan into place.

_A_ **8)** Some of the advocates of the plan originally voted against it.

The plan was originally voted against by some of its biggest advocates.

_P_ **9)** Prior to 1920, women in the United States were denied the right to vote.

Prior to 1920, the United States denied women the right to vote.

_A_ **10)** While they were on the raft, Huck and Jim shielded each other from the evils of civilization.

While they were on the raft, Huck and Jim were shielded from the evils of civilization.

Application & Enrichment
Verbs (Not Nouns) Are Action Words!

Active voice is preferred in most writing because it is more engaging to the reader. Specific situations do exist where passive voice is preferred, but in most cases, active voice should be your first choice. Sometimes, however, changing to active voice isn't enough. Look at the following sentences:

We went for a 20-mile hike.

We hiked twenty miles.

Even though the first sentence is technically active voice, the second is better for a couple of reasons.

• It is more efficient. We should always try to use as few words as possible to communicate.

• It is more engaging. The original verb, *went*, communicates some sort of motion, it's true. But *hiked* gives us a strong sense of **how** we *went*. We didn't *stroll*; we didn't *meander*; we didn't even *walk*. We *hiked!* To many of us, the verb *to hike* calls up a mental picture of rocks, boots, backpacks, and wilderness. Saying "*We went for a 20-mile hike*" communicates some of the same imagery, but the impact is delayed until the end of the sentence. *We hiked* creates a more direct response from the reader. They already have their picture of *hiking* in their mind before they even find out how long the hike was!

Many English nouns have a verb form and vice versa. When you are writing, watch out for helping verbs and see if your sentence has any action verbs hiding in nouns that you can use instead for a more powerful result.

We had a snack.

We snacked.

The baby was asleep.

The baby slept.

Note: Sometimes endings make it easy to find a noun that's hiding an action verb. The endings *-tion, -sion, -ance* and *-ment* are just a few of the endings that change a verb into a noun.

Examples: *complete + -tion = completion*

revise + -sion = revision

accept + -ance = acceptance

announce + ment = announcement

However, not all words make a change, so look at how the word is being used in a sentence to identify its job.

Examples: The dying fire gave off smoke. (*smoke* is a noun)

The dying fire smoked. (*smoked* is an action verb)

The clerk did the inventory count. (*count* is a noun)

The clerk counted the inventory. (*counted* is an action verb)

Directions

Find the action verb hiding in each of the following nouns. Write the verbs in their infinitive form, beginning with the word *to*.

Example: action   to act

1)   estimation   *to estimate*

2)   surprise   *to surprise*

3)   exhibition   *to exhibit*

4)   judgment   *to judge*

5)   excuse   *to excuse*

Directions

Write the noun form of each of the following action verbs. Look back at the note above and try possible endings if you need help:

6)   to dance   *dance*

7)   to measure   *measurement (or measure)*

8)   to place   *placement*

9)   to appear   *appearance*

10) to produce   *production*

Directions

Each of the sentences below includes an action verb that's hiding in a noun. Circle the noun and rewrite the sentence using the action verb. You can change other words if needed to make the best new sentence.

11) The teacher's (assessment) of the students was on Friday.

The teacher assessed the students on Friday.

12) I moved the (part) in my hair to the other side to see if I like it.

I parted my hair on the other side to see if I like it.

13) Aunt Shirley put the letter in the (mail.)

Aunt Shirley mailed the letter.

14) We gave our new kitten the (name) Puffy.

We named our new kitten Puffy.

15) The (highlight) of our visit was the beautiful mural.

The beautiful mural highlighted our visit.

Active & Passive Voice: Assessment

Directions

Identify whether each sentence is active or passive by writing **A** (active) or **P** (passive) in the space provided next to each sentence. Rewrite the sentence in the opposite voice on the lines provided. Include all of the elements of the original sentence. Because passive voice sentences may not include the doer, you might need to invent a doer to be the subject of your new active voice sentence.

Assign points as follows:

Correctly identifying the voice of the sentence = 1 point

Rewriting the sentence in the opposite voice = 3 points

Including all of the elements of the original sentence = 2 points

Total possible points for each sentence = 6 points

Rewritten sentences will vary; one possible answer has been provided.

_P_ **1)** Two key findings are indicated by the results of this test.
6

The results of this test indicate two key findings.

_A_ **2)** Researchers have found that heart disease is the leading cause of death in the USA.
6

Heart disease has been found to be the leading cause of death in the USA, according to research.

_A_ **3)** Why did you pack my stuff and leave it on the front lawn?
6

Why was my stuff packed and left on the front lawn?

_A_ **4)** Dr. Huang delivered the twins at 5:30 a.m. on May 5, 2020.
6

The twins were delivered by Dr. Huang at 5:30 a.m. on May 5, 2020.

___P___ **5)** Before he left the theater, the rock star was besieged by screaming fans.
6

Screaming fans besieged the rock star before he left the theater.

_____

___P___ **6)** A souvenir of her trip to give to her nephew was purchased by Nicki.
6

Nicki purchased a souvenir of her trip to give to her nephew.

_____

___A___ **7)** Before the test began, the students read the directions very carefully.
6

Before the test began, the directions were read very carefully by the students.

_____

___P___ **8)** The U.S. Constitution was signed on September 17, 1787.
6

The Founders signed the U.S. Constitution on September 17, 1787.

_____

___A___ **9)** Witnesses saw a man wearing a blue sweatshirt and jeans leaving the scene of the crime.
6

A man wearing a blue sweatshirt and jeans was seen leaving the scene of the crime by witnesses.

_____

___P___ **10)** As a result of our baseball game, Mrs. Hawkins's window was broken.
6

As a result of our baseball game, we broke Mrs. Hawkins's window.

_____

___P___ **11)** The girl sitting next to me was asked to share her notes from the prior lecture.
6

I asked the girl sitting next to me to share her notes from the prior lecture.

___A___ **12)** When the bell rang, the teacher told the class that they could leave.
6

When the bell rang, the class was told by the teacher that they could leave.

___A___ **13)** When were you planning to tell me about the broken vase?
6

When was I going to be told about the broken vase?

___A___ **14)** The man carrying the marked $100 bills finally admitted that he had stolen them.
6

The man carrying the marked $100 bills finally admitted that they were stolen.

___A___ **15)** The college athletic department has awarded James a full-ride scholarship for soccer.
6

A full-ride scholarship for soccer has been awarded to James by the college athletic department.

___P___ **16)** The Christmas money had been saved by the children all year long.
6

The children had been saving the Christmas money all year long.

_P_ **17)** Mrs. Dragonbottom's sarcasm had been patiently endured by the students for a month.

6

For a month, the students had patiently endured Mrs. Dragonbottom's sarcasm.

_A_ **18)** The drama class presented their spring play *The Crucible* for the student body.

6

The drama class's spring play The Crucible *was presented for the student body.*

_P_ **19)** My senior class trip began with a tour of D.C., which was taken by everybody in the group.

6

My senior class trip began with a tour of D.C., which everybody in the group took.

_P_ **20)** In ancient times, punctuation wasn't used, which makes their writing hard for us to read.

6

In ancient times, writers didn't use punctuation, which makes their writing hard for us to read.

$$\frac{96}{120} = 80\%$$ *Total Points*

120

Reinforcing Skills

Once Level 5 is completed, your student will have learned everything they need to know about grammar! Well, maybe not quite—there are always quirky rules or situations that will come up. But they will be armed with the knowledge they need to communicate their ideas clearly and effectively in any situation.

To keep their skills sharp, consider our *High School Grammar Reinforcements*. These self-corrected workbooks provide practice activities based on common high school literature themes. *World Authors*, *American Authors*, *British Authors*, and *Shakespeare's Plays* do not have to be used with literature, but they provide interesting background information on important authors and literary works. Complete one activity every two weeks during the school year to keep students at the top of their grammar game.

Index

Concepts are listed by lesson number.

*Indicates item is found in Application & Enrichment activity

Bibliography

Florey, Kitty Burns. Sister Bernadette's Barking Dog: The Quirky History and Lost Art of Diagramming Sentences. Orlando, FL: Harcourt, 2007.

Garner, Bryan A. Garner's Modern English Usage. Oxford: Oxford University Press, 2016.

Garner, Bryan A. The Chicago Guide to Grammar, Usage, and Punctuation. Chicago, IL: The University of Chicago Press, 2016.

Truss, Lynne. Eats, Shoots & Leaves: The Zero Tolerance Approach to Punctuation. London: Fourth Estate, 2009.